Mastering Coding Bat (Java)

Books by Ulm Publishing

Mastering Coding Bat (Java), Vol. 1: Basics
Mastering Coding Bat (Java), Vol. 2: Intermediate A
Mastering Coding Bat (Java), Vol. 3: Intermediate B
Mastering Coding Bat (Java), Vol. 4: Advanced

Mastering Coding Bat (Java)
Vol. 1: Basics

Gregor Ulm

Ulm Publishing

Copyright © 2018 by Gregor Ulm
http://www.gregorulm.com

Contents

Logic-1   251

Preface

In 2012, I published what was back then the first full set of solutions to Coding Bat (codingbat.com), both in Java and Python, on my website (gregorulm.com). To my great surprise, there has been substantial interest, judging from the number of visitors to my website, and the deluge of comments and emails I have received over the years. The solutions I developed and published online I originally wrote down very quickly, making sure they look clean enough and pass all test cases.

Over time, I noticed that people started to view my solutions as a work of reference, comparing their solutions to mine. That was not my intention at all. However, as I am convinced of the didactic value of Coding Bat, I would like to further expand on my online solutions in a series of books. The goal of these books is to introduce problems, describe how to tackle them, give hints and, which is of utmost interest to people learning how to program, present fully-worked solutions that discuss how you get from an idea to a working piece of code. That happens in a number of steps, which may include discussing alternative approaches. By doing so, a novice programmer will make two important realizations. The first one is that there are many valid solutions to a given problem, while the second one is that non-trivial programming tasks are performed incrementally, which may involve dismissing earlier attempts.

The expected reader is a novice programmer, probably a freshman in college. You may also be a high school student or a self-learner. By working through the books of this series, you will gain a very thorough understanding of elementary programming concepts. This will provide an excellent preparation for future projects, either during your university studies or at work.

If you work through those problems, you will be well on your way to becoming a competent programmer. Seeing that programming skills have become important in many industries, that time will be well-spent.

I found it very gratifying to witness the positive reception my Coding Bat solutions have found. I hope that my book series *Mastering Coding Bat* will find an equally warm reception.

Gregor Ulm
Gothenburg, Sweden

Introduction

The exercise set published on the Coding Bat website is an excellent tool for leaning how to program. According to its creator, Stanford professor Nick Parlante, the motivation behind that site is to gradually introduce people to solving increasingly difficult problems programmatically. This is a particularly useful tool for novices because the gap from not knowing much to having to solve the kind of problems you are confronted with in an introductory course in computer science can be quite intimidating.

Programming has become a highly useful skill. Even if you have no aspirations of becoming a full-time software developer, it is not at all implausible that your field, no matter what it is, can advance dramatically with increased automation. For the most part, that is what programmers do: they automate processes. Imagine how much more effective you could be at your job if you were able to automate or outsource everything that is tedious and repetitive! If you fully understand all the problems on Coding Bat, you are well on the way of joining the automators, if you so desire.

With this book, the goal is to dissect every problem in the four Coding Bat sections *Warmup-1*, *String-1*, *Array-1*, and *Logic-1*. Those sections introduce basic operations, which are the bread and butter of programming. They gradually introduce new concepts, but not too many of them. There is also a significant amount of problems that are variations of previous ones, which allow you to solidify your knowledge.

This book is primarily for everyone who has encountered Coding Bat and would like to get a bit more hand-holding, better guid-

3

ance, or some help with understanding the various problems. You could be a high school student, or maybe you are enrolled in college. You may even be an autodidact. No matter your role, you may have encountered the problem that even books and other materials that are supposedly written for beginners assume a significant amount of knowledge. Even worse, many of those books are incredibly, incredibly verbose. In contrast, this book presents you with the meat of programming. If you make it through it, you will become a better programmer.

How to use this book

View this book as your personal tutor who guides you through Coding Bat. The presentation of each problem has a fixed format. We start with the *problem description*, which also contains a skeleton of the code, i.e. a function signature. It is your task to come up with the body of the function. There are many ways to skin a cat, and there are at least as many ways to solving problems programmatically. However, some approaches keep you from learning certain skills. Thus, this book lists the *tools* you can use for solving a given problem. It may be tempting to just use an in-built method in Java that does what you are supposed to write code for, but if you do that, you are not going to progress much.

In order to guide you in the right directions, the *hints* section provides a few pointers. Depending on the problem, those can be substantial or almost nonexistent. Sometimes it is just a reference to a previous and similar problem. This is followed by the normally only sparsely commented *solution*, which shows one possible solution to the problem. It will be correct, but it may not be the most elegant one. In contrast, the optional *discussion* section highlights different approaches or presents variations. Some problems come with a very extensive discussion section that contains several alternative solutions.

Treat this book essentially as very extensive commentary. I would suggest that you work through it sequentially as the problems tend to increase in difficulty. If you jump around and get stuck, you may only get needlessly frustrated. For each problem, start by reading the problem description. Then look at the code skeleton. Instead of writing code on the Coding Bat website, however, I would like you to use pencil and paper. Yes, you read that correctly. Before starting to type, write code by hand and try to come up with a solution that is as close to working code as possible. By not writing executable Java code straight away you will not get tempted to, for instance, guessing and using the website as some kind of feedback generator that helps you to gradually figure out the solution. Instead, with your pencil in hand, you figure out the problem before writing any code on the computer. If you cannot do that, then you may need to think harder about the problem. As you get more experienced, you may want to skip writing code down on paper first. However, if you find yourself changing your code too much, then you probably need to spend more time figuring out the solution in your head first.

Once you are content with the code you have written down on paper, go to the Coding Bat website. Enter your solution and execute the code. Fix syntactic errors if there are any. (Optional: if you get stuck, use my hints.) After you have solved the problem correctly, look at my solution and the discussion. Compare your solution with mine. Make sure you understand every single line in both your code and my solutions as well as all the variations.

Lastly, I would recommend you work steadily through this book. Do at least one or two problems every day, but ideally more. I think you should be able to do at least five problems a day very comfortably.

Warmup-1

sleepIn

Problem

This problem introduces you to basic operations on truth values, i.e. true and false. We begin by restating the problem definition. Your task is to write the body of a function sleepIn that takes two arguments, weekday, a boolean value, and vacation, likewise a boolean value. Both arguments are taken at face value, e.g. the value weekday is true if it is true that the current day is a weekday, and so on. The goal is to produce an output consisting of one boolean value. The conditions are as follows: If weekday is false, then the return value is true. If vacation is true, then the return value is true. In all other cases, return false. The code skeleton is given in Listing 1.

```
1  public boolean sleepIn(boolean weekday, boolean vacation) {
2  // your code here
3  }
```

Listing 1: sleepIn – skeleton

Tools

This problem can be solved by using if-statements as well as the boolean operators for *not* (!), *and* (&&), and *or* (||). In addition, you may want to use the equality operator (==).

Hints

This is a straightforward problem. Start with translating the conditions listed in the problem statement into conditional expressions. Afterwards, think of ways to simplify the code.

Solution

With some experience, you will be able to directly translate the problem specification to a very concise solution like the one-liner shown in Listing 2.

```
1 public boolean sleepIn(boolean weekday, boolean vacation) {
2   return !weekday || vacation;
3 }
```

Listing 2: sleepIn – solution

Discussion

The function sleepIn takes two boolean values as inputs. Since there are two boolean values and each boolean value can be either true or false, there are a total of four possible conditions. Thus, a first possible solution might consist of encoding all four possibilities, as shown by the code in Listing 3. Please keep in mind that this is not particularly elegant code. We are going to gradually refine it.

```
1  public boolean sleepIn(boolean weekday, boolean vacation) {
2    if ((weekday == true) && (vacation == true)) {
3      return true;
4    }
5    if ((weekday == true) && (vacation == false)) {
6      return false;
7    }
8    if ((weekday == false) && (vacation == true)) {
9      return true;
10   }
11   if ((weekday == false) && (vacation == false)) {
12     return true;
13   }
14   return false;
15 }
```

Listing 3: sleepIn – variation 1

A few comments are in order. First, I consider it good practice to include parentheses when using boolean operators. The equality operator has a higher *precedence* than the *and* and *or* operators, which means that the parentheses around expressions such as (weekday == true) are not necessary. However, they can be helpful when reading code.

Second, you may have noticed that there is a final return-clause, which seems to be superfluous since we cover all four possible cases with our code. However, the Java compiler cannot infer that we exhaustively cover all cases. It therefore insists on a separate return-statement. In this case, it does not matter which boolean value we return as the default value as the final statement is unreachable and can therefore never be executed. Generally speaking, when the default return value can be reached, you would want to pick a safe default choice. This depends on the context. In our example, it is generally safe not to sleep in, while sleeping in when you are not on vacation may have negative consequences. Thus, `false` is the safer choice.

Third, it is generally good practice to not omit curly braces when the body of an if-statement is only one line long. It does not matter in this case, but in practice, omitting curly braces is a very common source of errors. It is an easy mistake to make to add an additional line to the body of an if-clause, which is not separated with parentheses. This means that the added line will be executed in any case, and not just when the condition that is checked by the if-statement is true.

The code example above is quite awkward, so let us continue by cleaning it up. For instance, `weekday == true` can be rewritten as simply `weekday`. Similarly, `weekday == false` is equivalent to `!weekday`. Thus, the next version of our solution is significantly shorter. Please refer to Listing 4.

```
1 public boolean sleepIn(boolean weekday, boolean vacation) {
2   if (weekday && vacation) {
3     return true;
4   }
5   if (weekday && !vacation) {
6     return false;
7   }
8   if (!weekday && vacation) {
9     return true;
10   }
11   if (!weekday && !vacation) {
12     return true;
13   }
14   return false;
15 }
```

Listing 4: sleepIn – variation 2

This looks a lot better already. Now, if you squint a little bit, you may realize something interesting: of the four conditions, only one leads us to return true. The others return false. Consequently, we can collapse all cases that return true into one single case, as shown in Listing 5.

```
1 public boolean sleepIn(boolean weekday, boolean vacation) {
2   if (weekday && !vacation) {
3     return false;
4   }
5   return true;
6 }
```

Listing 5: sleepIn – variation 3

The previous solution is fine. However, you could improve it further and turn it into a one-liner due to the fact that the boolean values we want to return can be arrived at directly by evaluating an expression. This is shown in Listing 6.

```
1 public boolean sleepIn(boolean weekday, boolean vacation) {
2   return !(weekday && !vacation);
3 }
```

Listing 6: sleepIn – variation 4

The expression seen in Listing 6 is correct, but unnecessarily complicated as it will take you a moment or two to sort out the negations in your head while reading it. However, there is an equivalent expression that is more readable. Please refer to Listing 7. If you are an experienced programmer, this could well have been your first and only attempt.

```
1  public boolean sleepIn(boolean weekday, boolean vacation) {
2    return !weekday || vacation;
3  }
```

Listing 7: sleepIn – variation 5

This successive rewriting of code that behaves the same, which you have just witnessed, is sometimes called *refactoring*.[1] It is common practice in professional software development as well, where the first version you write is often code that meets the required specification, even though it may hardly be ideal. Afterwards, you may want to clean it up to make it more concise, more readable, or faster. However, I would advise you not to aim for the most concise code if it ends up looking rather convoluted.

---

[1]In my opinion, the term refactoring is rather pretentious, as are so many others in this field. It would not be quite as bad if it was a fitting metaphor, but rewriting code has very little to do with, for instance, factoring a mathematical expression differently. (I consider it adequate to refer to certain actions as *factoring out*, for instance when using a variable or a helper function to avoid repetition.) Other terms I consider highly dubious if not downright harmful are *code smell* for poorly written code that is hard to maintain or *bug* instead of mistake or error. Those two have in common that the chosen metaphors make it sound as if the programmer is not truly responsible for the poor work he has produced. Instead, due to exposure to sunlight, code began to smell, then to rot – yes, some programmers speak of *code rot*) – until it finally attracted bugs and other vermin. Intellectual honesty in software development starts with not using any of those terms.

monkeyTrouble

Problem

The exercise `monkeyTrouble` is very similar to `sleepIn`. It takes two boolean values as arguments, `aSmile` and `bSmile` and returns `true` if both arguments are true or if both arguments are false. Otherwise, it returns `false`. Let us reformulate the conditions: If `aSmile` is `false` and `bSmile` is `false`, return `true`. If `aSmile` is `true` and `bSmile` is `true`, return `true`. Otherwise, return `false`.

The code skeleton is provided in Listing 8.

```
1  public boolean monkeyTrouble(boolean aSmile,
2                               boolean bSmile) {
3    // your code here
4  }
```

Listing 8: monkeyTrouble – skeleton

Tools

This problem can be solved by using conditional expressions as well as the boolean operators for *not* (!), *and* (&&), and *or* (||). In addition, you may want to use the equality operator (==).

Hints

Look at the restated conditions above and translate them directly into Java.

Solution

A perfectly adequate solution is shown in Listing 9. However, there is a more elegant solution, which is revealed further below.

```java
public boolean monkeyTrouble(boolean aSmile,
                             boolean bSmile) {
  return (aSmile && bSmile) || (!aSmile && !bSmile);
}
```

Listing 9: monkeyTrouble – solution

Discussion

Our approach to solving monkeyTrouble is similar to what you have seen in the discussion of problem sleepIn. This means that we start by listing all four cases, which you can see in Listing 10. Overall, we speed things up a little bit, though.

```java
public boolean monkeyTrouble(boolean aSmile,
                             boolean bSmile) {
  if (aSmile && bSmile) {
    return true;
  }
  if (aSmile && !bSmile) {
    return false;
  }
  if (!aSmile && bSmile) {
    return false;
  }
  if (!aSmile && !bSmile) {
    return true;
  }
  return false;
}
```

Listing 10: monkeyTrouble – variation 1

To simplify this code, combine either all conditions that return true or all conditions that return false. In the following, the conditions that return true are retained. All other conditions are captured in the final return statement, which returns false. Have a look at the code in Listing 11.

```
1  public boolean monkeyTrouble(boolean aSmile,
2                               boolean bSmile) {
3    if (aSmile && bSmile) {
4      return true;
5    }
6    if (!aSmile && !bSmile) {
7      return true;
8    }
9    return false;
10 }
```

Listing 11: monkeyTrouble – variation 2

You can probably see that the remaining two if-statements can be combined by using the or-operator. This leads to the code shown in Listing 12.

```
1  public boolean monkeyTrouble(boolean aSmile,
2                               boolean bSmile) {
3    if ((aSmile && bSmile) || (!aSmile && !bSmile)) {
4      return true;
5    }
6    return false;
7  }
```

Listing 12: monkeyTrouble – variation 3

By now, you may consider such code awkward as the if-statement is redundant. Instead, it is possible to directly check whether the given condition is true, as shown in Listing 13.

```
1  public boolean monkeyTrouble(boolean aSmile,
2                               boolean bSmile) {
3    return (aSmile && bSmile) || (!aSmile && !bSmile);
4  }
```

Listing 13: monkeyTrouble – variation 4

Sometimes, it is possible to simplify a problem by an insight into its underlying structure. In our case, think about how the two arguments relate to each other. You may notice that the check encoded in the function body above is about determining whether aSmile and bSmile have the same value. If you make that realization, you will be able to come up with a neat and elegant solution that encapsulates that insight. Have a look at the code in Listing 14.

```
1  public boolean monkeyTrouble(boolean aSmile,
2                               boolean bSmile) {
3    return aSmile == bSmile;
4  }
```

Listing 14: *monkeyTrouble – variation 5*

sumDouble

Problem

The problem sumDouble introduces arithmetic operators. Your task is to write a function that takes two integers a and b as arguments and returns twice their sum if a equals b. Otherwise, return their sum. Again, let us reformulate the conditions: If a is equal to b, then return 2 * (a + b). Otherwise, return a + b. The code skeleton is provided in Listing 15.

```
1 public int sumDouble(int a, int b) {
2   // your code here
3 }
```

Listing 15: sumDouble – skeleton

Tools

For this problem, your tools are conditional statements, the equality operator (==), and the arithmetic operators for addition (+) as well as multiplication (*).

Hints

This is a very easy problem. If you are stuck, then translate the reformulated conditions of the problem, which are given above, into Java.

Solution

A straightforward solution is given below, in Listing 16. In the subsequent discussion, you will see how to express this more concisely.

```
1 public int sumDouble(int a, int b) {
2   if (a == b) {
3     return 2 * (a + b);
4   } else {
5     return a + b;
6   }
7 }
```

Listing 16: *sumDouble* – solution

Discussion

The problem sumDouble is straightforward. There are two parts in the problem statement. The first one states to return the sum of two values a and b. Let us stop reading right there and code this up. See Listing 17. Of course, the code does not yet take all cases into account, but it is a start. Run it on codingbat.com and notice that it already passes some test cases. Do not scoff at this step, because for more complicated problems, it is viable to tackle sub-problems one by one and verify their correctness before moving on.

```
1 public int sumDouble(int a, int b) {
2   return a + b;
3 }
```

Listing 17: *sumDouble* – variation 1 (incomplete)

Afterwards, we only need to add the second requirement, namely that the return value needs to be doubled if the two input values are identical. Listing 18 shows the corresponding code. I am using a variable res to store the sum of the values a and b because this makes the code a bit more concise. It is partly a matter of taste. However, in larger programs, it may happen that repetitive code leads to repeated computation of values. In those cases, precomputing results leads to better performance.

19

```
1 public int sumDouble(int a, int b) {
2   int res = a + b;
3   if (a == b) {
4     res = 2 * res;
5   }
6   return res;
7 }
```

Listing 18: sumDouble – variation 2

As an alternative to the code given in Listing 18, you can of course encode the second condition with an else-clause, which I have done in the suggested solution earlier. However, there is a more elegant way of expressing this by using the so-called *ternary operator*. This is a special operator that takes three elements and can be used to shorten conditional statements. I recommend that you use it only when it clearly improves readability, as it can lead to code that is difficult to untangle, particularly if you nest multiple ternary operators. For our current problem, though, there is no downside, so we use that operator to shorten the code. See Listing 19.

```
1 public int sumDouble(int a, int b) {
2   return (a == b) ? (2 * (a + b)) : (a + b);
3 }
```

Listing 19: sumDouble – variation 3

Some of the parentheses are superfluous. However, they improve readability. For instance, compare the code in Listing 19 with a new variation, shown in Listing 20, that is more concise and, arguably, more difficult to read.

```
1 public int sumDouble(int a, int b) {
2   return a == b ? 2 * (a + b) : a + b;
3 }
```

Listing 20: sumDouble – variation 4

As we have seen earlier, it can be more elegant as well as efficient to remove repetition. Thus, since the computation a + b takes place at least once in each of the two cases, we can factor it out. We can also store the computation in a separate variable so that we do not have to repeat it. In Listing 21 we return the sum of a + b sum plus either the sum of a + b or 0.

```java
public int sumDouble(int a, int b) {
  int sum = a + b;
  return sum + (a == b ? sum : 0);
}
```

Listing 21: *sumDouble – variation 5*

diff21

Problem

In `diff21`, the goal is to straightforwardly check a condition. In this problem, comparison operators other than the one for equality are introduced. The function `diff21` takes an integer n as input. If n is greater than 21, then return double the absolute difference of n and 21. Otherwise, return the absolute difference of n and 21. The code skeleton is provided in Listing 22.

```
1 public int diff21(int n) {
2 // your code here
3 }
```

Listing 22: *diff21 – skeleton*

Tools

For this problem you may use a conditional statement. You will also need the comparison operator for greater-than (>) and basic arithmetic operators. The inbuilt method `Math.abs` should not be used.

Hints

Start by reformulating the conditions mentioned in the problem description: If n is greater than 21, return twice the absolute difference of n and 21. Otherwise, return the absolute difference of n and 21.

Solution

A simple solution, following the outline provided in the hints above, is shown in Listing 23.

```
1  public int diff21(int n) {
2    if (n > 21) {
3        return 2 * (n - 21);
4    } else {
5      int tmp = n - 21;
6      if (tmp < 0) {
7        return -tmp;
8      } else {
9        return tmp;
10     }
11   }
12 }
```

Listing 23: diff21 – solution

Discussion

We will develop this solution step by step. The first condition is straightforward to encode: If n is greater than 21, we return twice the absolute difference of n and 21. Also, note that if n is greater than 21, then n – 21 is always greater than 0. An incomplete solution, which already passes some of the test cases, is shown in Listing 24.

```
1  public int diff21(int n) {
2    if (n > 21) {
3      return 2 * (n - 21);
4    } else {
5      return 0;
6    }
7  }
```

Listing 24: diff21 – variation 1 (incomplete)

Afterwards, we add the second condition. To make the code a bit more concise, we store the result of the computation n – 21 in a temporary variable, tmp. If tmp is less than zero, we need to negate that variable, because the absolute difference is always nonnegative. The full code is given in Listing 25.

```
1  public int diff21(int n) {
2    if (n > 21) {
3        return 2 * (n - 21);
4    } else {
5      int tmp = n - 21;
6      if (tmp < 0) {
7        return -tmp;
8      } else {
9        return tmp;
10      }
11    }
12  }
```

Listing 25: diff21 – variation 2

The code in Listing 25 would benefit from using the ternary operator, which you have encountered earlier. Thus, a more concise version is given in Listing 26.

```
1  public int diff21(int n) {
2    if (n > 21) {
3        return 2 * (n - 21);
4    } else {
5      int tmp = n - 21;
6      return (tmp < 0) ? -tmp : tmp;
7    }
8  }
```

Listing 26: diff21 – variation 3

A neat variation consists of factoring out the value tmp and multiplying it with −1 if it is below zero. See Listing 27 for that approach.

```
1  public int diff21(int n) {
2    if (n > 21) {
3        return 2 * (n - 21);
4    } else {
5      int tmp = n - 21;
6      return tmp * (tmp < 0 ? -1 : 1);
7    }
8  }
```

Listing 27: diff21 – variation 4

parrotTrouble

Problem

In parrotTrouble you will work with boolean values and comparisons. The function takes two arguments, a boolean talking and an integer hour. The goal is to return true if talking is true and hour is either less than 7 or greater than 20. See Listing 28 for the code skeleton.

```
1 public boolean parrotTrouble(boolean talking, int hour) {
2 // your code here
3 }
```

Listing 28: parrotTrouble – skeleton

Tools

For this problem, you can use boolean operators, comparison operators, and conditional statements.

Hints

Start by reformulating the conditions in the problem descriptions: If talking is true and hour is less than 7, return true. If talking is true and hour is greater than 20, return true. Otherwise, return false.

Solution

A straightforward solution, modeled after the hints, is given in Listing 29. Of course, those nested if-statements are a bit unsightly. Further below, we will see how to structure this code in a different way.

```
1 public boolean parrotTrouble(boolean talking, int hour) {
2   if (talking && hour < 7) {
3     return true;
4   } else if (talking && hour > 20) {
5     return true;
6   } else {
7   return false;
8   }
9 }
```

Listing 29: parrotTrouble – solution

Discussion

Using the conditions stated in the hints section above, we start with a very straightforward translation into Java as seen in Listing 30. This is already more readable than the code shown in Listing 29 as we have gotten rid of the nested if-statement.

```
1 public boolean parrotTrouble(boolean talking, int hour) {
2   if (talking && hour < 7) {
3     return true;
4   }
5   if (talking && hour > 20) {
6     return true;
7   }
8   return false;
9 }
```

Listing 30: parrotTrouble – variation 1

The two if-statements can be combined with an or-operator. See Listing 31 for the code.

```
1 public boolean parrotTrouble(boolean talking, int hour) {
2   if ((talking && hour < 7) || (talking && hour > 20)) {
3     return true;
4   }
5   return false;
6 }
```

Listing 31: parrotTrouble – variation 2)

At this point, it should be obvious that you can simplify the code even further. In fact, whenever you encounter an expression of the structure in Listing 32, you can simplify it to return condition right away. I have encountered the verbose version with the redundant conditional statement in code written by professional software developers on more than a few occasions. It is not wrong, but it is unsightly and arguably tasteless.

```
1 if (condition) {
2   return true;
3 }
4 return false;
```

Listing 32: Redundant if-statement

Let us return to parrotTrouble. Seeing that the expression we have is similar to the pattern just mentioned, a more concise version of our solution can be found easily. This is given in Listing 33, which is perfectly adequate.

```
1 public boolean parrotTrouble(boolean talking, int hour) {
2   return (talking && hour < 7) || (talking && hour > 20);
3 }
```

Listing 33: parrotTrouble – variation 3

Those of you who are more comfortable with boolean operators probably see that there is room for further simplification. It is redundant to check whether talking is true in both condition because we could as well just check it one single time. Consequently, we can factor our the first condition. That approach is reflected in the code in Listing 34.

```
1 public boolean parrotTrouble(boolean talking, int hour) {
2   return talking && (hour < 7 || hour > 20);
3 }
```

Listing 34: parrotTrouble – variation 4

makes10

Problem

The problem makes10 only uses constructs we have seen already. You are given a function that takes two integers a and b as its arguments. Return true if one of them is equal to 10 or if their sum is equal to 10. Otherwise, return false. The code skeleton is provided in Listing 35.

```
1 public boolean makes10(int a, int b) {
2 // your code here
3 }
```

Listing 35: makes10 – skeleton

Tools

For this problem you can use conditional statements, boolean operators, arithmetic operators, and the equality operator.

Hints

Start by reformulating the conditions in the problem description, and translate them into Java code. You will have to express the following conditions in code: If a == 10, return true. If b == 10, return true. If a + b == 10, return true. Otherwise, return false.

Solution

A straightforward solution, following the hints given above, is given in Listing 36.

```java
public boolean makes10(int a, int b) {
  if (a == 10) {
    return true;
  } else if (b == 10) {
    return true;
  } else if (a + b == 10) {
    return true;
  } else {
    return false;
  }
}
```

Listing 36: makes10 – solution

Discussion

The sample solution given in Listing 36 is a good starting point as it is a direct translation of the conditions given earlier. It is by no means a particularly concise solution, though. In order to improve the code, we therefore combine the first two conditions into one clause and turn the final if-clause into a simple return-statement. Please refer to Listing 37.

```java
public boolean makes10(int a, int b) {
  if (a == 10 || b == 10) {
    return true;
  } else if (a + b == 10) {
    return true;
  }
  return false;
}
```

Listing 37: makes10 – variation 1

As a novice Java programmer, you may not have encountered that you can chain boolean operators. In our case, the remaining two conditions can therefore be collapsed into just one. This is shown in Listing 38.

31

```
1  public boolean makes10(int a, int b) {
2    if (a == 10 || b == 10 || (a + b == 10)) {
3      return true;
4    }
5    return false;
6  }
```

Listing 38: makes10 – variation 2

Do you notice how the code in Listing 38 can be simplified even further? Again, this is a case of a superfluous conditional statement. This enables us to write a one-line solution, given in Listing 39.

```
1  public boolean makes10(int a, int b) {
2    return a == 10 || b == 10 || a + b == 10;
3  }
```

Listing 39: makes10 – variation 3

nearHundred

Problem

The aim of the function `nearHundred` is to take a number n and determine if it is within 10 of either 100 or 200. This problem introduces working with in-built methods, in this case `Math.abs`. The code skeleton is given in Listing 40.

```
1 public boolean nearHundred(int n) {
2 // your code here
3 }
```

Listing 40: `nearHundred` – skeleton

Tools

For this problem you can use conditional statements, boolean operators, arithmetic operators, and the equality operator. In addition, you are free to use the inbuilt method `Math.abs`.

Hints

This is a very straightforward problem, which should not require much hand-holding. In order to figure out whether n is within 10 of any number x, take the absolute difference of those two numbers and check whether the result is less than or equal to 10. Breaking down the problem statement into three different cases, we get the following: If n is within 10 of 100, return `true`. If n is within 10 of 200, return `true`. Otherwise, return `false`.

Solution

A valid yet awkward solution based on the hints section is given in Listing 41.

```java
public boolean nearHundred(int n) {
  if (Math.abs(100 - n) <= 10) {
    return true;
  }
  if (Math.abs(200 - n) <= 10) {
    return true;
  }
  return false;
}
```

Listing 41: nearHundred – solution

Discussion

Since this is a very straight-forward problem, there is not much to develop here. Starting with the solution in Listing 41, one could combine both if-clauses into one, like in the code in Listing 42.

```java
public boolean nearHundred(int n) {
  if ((Math.abs(100 - n) <= 10)
      || (Math.abs(200 - n) <= 10)) {
    return true;
  }
  return false;
}
```

Listing 42: nearHundred – variation 1

By now, you should immediately notice that the resulting if-clause is superfluous, which leads to even shorter code. Please refer to Listing 43.

```java
public boolean nearHundred(int n) {
  return Math.abs(100 - n) <= 10
         || Math.abs(200 - n) <= 10;
}
```

Listing 43: nearHundred – variation 2

While this is a more concise solution, it is arguably less readable than the version we started out with, which was given in Listing 41. This points to an important issue in software development: there is normally no ideal solution. Instead, you have to consider trade-offs. Minimizing the number of lines at the cost of readability is not necessarily the best approach in that regard.

posNeg

Problem

The function `posNeg` takes two integers `a` and `b` as well as a boolean `negative` as its input. If `negative` is `true`, the function checks whether both a and b are negative. If `negative` is `false`, on the other hand, this function checks whether one of a and b is negative. The function signature is given in Listing 44 below. This problem deserves some attention as there is a long obvious solution, but also a very elegant and concise one that is based on domain knowledge.

```
1 public boolean posNeg(int a, int b, boolean negative) {
2 // your code here
3 }
```

Listing 44: posNeg – skeleton

Tools

For this problem you can use conditional statements, boolean operators, arithmetic operators, and comparison operators.

Hints

Breaking down the problem description, we arrive at the following conditions: If `negative` is `false`, return `true` if exactly one of a and b is negative. If `negative` is `true`, return `true` if both a and b are negative. Otherwise, return `false`. However, there is a more elegant solution, which depends on the properties of a and b. You may not see this immediately, but it is well worth thinking about it for a while before working through the discussion further below.

Solution

A straightforward solution to posNeg is given in Listing 45 below. It is directly modeled after the hints subsection above.

```
1  public boolean posNeg(int a, int b, boolean negative) {
2    if (!negative) {
3      return (a < 0 && b > 0) || (a > 0 && b < 0);
4    } else {
5      return (a < 0 && b < 0);
6    }
7  }
```

Listing 45: posNeg – solution

Discussion

The solution given in Listing 45 is perfectly adequate and very readable. It could be further condensed by using the ternary operator. Yet, this would hardly improve readability. There is another way of tackling this problem, though, which depends on thinking about the arguments a and b. We know that they are integers that are either positive or negative, which excludes the number 0. Keeping this in mind, can you think of a simple way to determine whether exactly one of a and b is negative? As a hint, try using a standard mathematical operator and see what you can come up with.

Could you figure it out? If not, then think about the result of multiplying a by b. What happens if exactly one of these numbers is negative? In that case, the result is negative. Thus, we can simplify the previous solution. See the code in Listing 46.

```
1  public boolean posNeg(int a, int b, boolean negative) {
2    if (!negative) {
3      return a * b < 0;
4    } else {
5      return a < 0 && b < 0;
6    }
7  }
```

Listing 46: posNeg – variation 1

This looks a lot better already, but we are not done yet. Now, look at the else-clause. Can you think of a way to determine whether both a and b are negative? If your initial thought was to multiply them and check whether the result is positive, then consider what happens if both a and b are positive. The result is positive, just like if both numbers were negative, so this is not a valid check. Instead, to determine if both a and b are negative, check whether their sum is negative. Obviously, if a is negative and b is negative, then a + b is negative as well. This leads to a further simplification. Refer to the code in Listing 47.

```
1  public boolean posNeg(int a, int b, boolean negative) {
2    if (!negative) {
3      return a * b < 0;
4    } else {
5      return a + b < 0;
6    }
7  }
```

Listing 47: posNeg – variation 2

At this point, seeing how short the various checks are, we can easily use the ternary operator and make the code even more concise. Also, we change the order of the checks, which removes the negation in the if-clause. See Listing 48 for the final code. Two of the statements have been put in parentheses in order to improve readability.

```
1  public boolean posNeg(int a, int b, boolean negative) {
2    return negative ? (a + b < 0) : (a * b < 0);
3  }
```

Listing 48: posNeg – variation 3

notString

Problem

In the problem `notString`, we encounter strings. The function takes a string `str` as an argument and adds `"not "` to it, including a space at the end. However, this only happens if the string `str` does not start with `"not"`. If it does start with `"not"`, then return `str` unchanged. See Listing 49 for the code skeleton.

```
1 public String notString(String str) {
2 // your code here
3 }
```

Listing 49: `notString` – skeleton

Tools

You can use conditional statements, comparison operators, boolean operators, the string concatenation operator as well as the string methods `length`, `substring`, and `equals`.

Hints

The problem description does not indicate that there is an issue with the method `substring`: If the string you are applying this method to is not within the boundaries of the substring you have specifed, Java throws an exception, i.e. your program crashes. Consequently, you first need to check the length of the string. In case the string `str` is of the correct length, check if the first three characters of it equal `"not"`.

Solution

Based on the hints provided above, one possible solution is given in Listing 50. We systematically perform the required checks. If any of the checks fail, we know that we need to prepend the string with "not ". Obviously, if the string is not at least three characters long, it cannot start with "not". Therefore, we can return a new string, consisting of the input string `str`, prepended with " not". We also do this if `str` is at least three characters long, but does not start with "not". Otherwise, we return `str`.

```java
public String notString(String str) {
  if (str.length() >= 3) {
    String prefix = str.substring(0, 3);
    if (prefix.equals("not")) {
      return str;
    }
  }
  return "not " + str;
}
```

Listing 50: notString – solution

Discussion

Let us start by tackling this problem case by case. The first important observation is that if the input string `str` is less than three characters long, we have to prepend it with "not ". After all, we are checking if `str` starts with "not", and if it is not at least three characters long, it is not possible that it could start with that word. If the function `notString` has not returned after the first if-clause, we perform a second check, based on the first three letters of the string. If that substring equals "not", we return the string `str` unchanged. Finally, if the function still has not returned, we return a new string, made of `str` and a prepended string "not ". The corresponding code is provided in Listing 51. We will look at a few more variations further below.

43

```
1  public String notString(String str) {
2    if (str.length() < 3) {
3      return "not " + str;
4    }
5    if (str.substring(0, 3).equals("not")) {
6      return str;
7    }
8    return "not " + str;
9  }
```

Listing 51: notString – variation 1

In order to further simplify the code, it would be helpful if the first if-clause could be modified so that it returns str. For this, we need to combine the two if-clauses, for example by nesting, as shown in Listing 52.

```
1  public String notString(String str) {
2    if (str.length() >= 3) {
3      if (str.substring(0, 3).equals("not")) {
4        return str;
5      }
6    }
7    return "not " + str;
8  }
```

Listing 52: notString – variation 2

We can condense the code further by removing the nested if-clause, as shown in Listing 53. I would not recommend turning the resulting code into a one-liner by using the ternary operator as the resulting code would be difficult to read.

```
1  public String notString(String str) {
2    if (str.length() >= 3
3        && str.substring(0, 3).equals("not")) {
4      return str;
5    }
6    return "not " + str;
7  }
```

Listing 53: notString – variation 3

missingChar

Problem

The function `missingChar` takes a string `str` and an integer n.
Return a new string that is missing the character at position n in
the string `str`. The input string contains at least n characters.
Refer to Listing 54 for the code skeleton.[2]

```java
public String missingChar(String str, int n) {
// your code here
}
```

Listing 54: missingChar – skeleton

Tools

This problem requires the use of the string method `substring`
as well as the string concatenation operator (+).

Hints

The key to solving this problem is selecting two substrings, such
that the character at position n is not part of either substring.
Keep in mind that there is some potential confusion as in Java
the first character in a string is at position 0. In this exercise,
n specifies the position in the zero-indexed input string, not the
position you would arrive at when counting from 1.

---

[2]On a side note, I think this problem should have been modified or
placed before `notString` as that problem introduces out-of-bound errors,
while this problem provides input that is valid. For instance, the empty
string as input would cause an out-of-bounds error, but it is excluded from
the set of inputs.

Solution

The simplest solution to this problem consists of selecting a substring containing all characters before the character at position n as well as a substring selecting all characters after position n. See Listing 55 for the code.

```
1  public String missingChar(String str, int n) {
2    return str.substring(0, n) + str.substring(n + 1);
3  }
```

Listing 55: missingChar – solution

Discussion

Start by extracting a substring that contains all characters up to position n in string str. You do this by calling the method substring with 0 as the first argument and n as the second argument. The second argument specifies the first character that is not part of the substring. In order to extract the substring after position n, it is sufficient to call substring with the argument n + 1. If you call substring with only one argument, you extract a substring from the indicated position all the way to the end of the string. The code in Listing 56 reflects this approach. Of course, you can just as well replace front and back in the return-statement with the actual computation, as was shown in Listing 55 previously.

```
1  public String missingChar(String str, int n) {
2    String front = str.substring(0, n);
3    String back  = str.substring(n + 1);
4    return front + back;
5  }
```

Listing 56: missingChar – variation

frontBack

Problem

For `frontBack`, write a function that takes as an input a string `str` and returns a string which is identical to `str`, except that the first and last character are swapped. The input string may be empty. See Listing 57 for the code skeleton.

```
1 public String frontBack(String str) {
2 // your code here
3 }
```

Listing 57: frontBack – skeleton

Tools

You can use a conditional statement, comparison operators, the string concatenation operator and the following string methods: `length`, `charAt`, and `substring`.

Hints

While I would consider the empty string invalid input, due to the fact that the empty string does not have a first or last character, it is part of the test cases on Coding Bat. Thus, you have to consider what should happen in two corner cases, the empty string and a string of length 1. With a string of length 1, the first character is also the last character, so you can return the string unchanged.

Solution

We first take care of both corner cases by processing all strings that are not at least of length 2. Afterwards, we construct a new string by extracting the first and last character as well as a substring containing the first to the second-to-last character. Refer to Listing 58 for the code.

```java
public String frontBack(String str) {
  if (str.length() <= 1) {
    return str;
  }
  return str.charAt(str.length() - 1)
         + str.substring(1, str.length() - 1)
         + str.charAt(0);
}
```

Listing 58: frontBack – solution

Discussion

Let us use the code in Listing 58 as a starting point. First, return the input string `str` if `str` is not at least two characters long. This takes care of input strings of length 0 and 1. Obviously, there are no strings with a negative length. Afterwards, we construct the result for the remaining cases. For readability, you may also want to name the parts of the final string. The corresponding code is given in Listing 59.

```java
public String frontBack(String str) {
  if (str.length() <= 1) {
    return str;
  }
  char   first = str.charAt(str.length() - 1);
  char   last  = str.charAt(0);
  String mid   = str.substring(1, str.length() - 1);
  return first + mid + last;
}
```

Listing 59: frontBack – variation 1

You may notice that we repeatedly call the string method `length`. This is bad practice. In this example, it does not make much of a difference. However, in production code you would not want to repeat expensive computations. Thus, we introduce a

49

helper variable `len` to clean up the code. Refer to the code in Listing 60 for that variation.

```java
public String frontBack(String str) {
  int len = str.length();
  if (len <= 1) {
    return str;
  }
  char   first = str.charAt(len - 1);
  char   last  = str.charAt(0);
  String mid   = str.substring(1, len - 1);
  return first + mid + last;
}
```

Listing 60: frontBack – variation 2

front3

Problem

The function `front3` takes a string `str` as input. For this function, we define *front* to mean the first three characters of a string. However, if the string has a length of less than 3, front refers to the entire string. The goal is to return a new string that contains the front of the string three times in a row. See Listing 61 for the code skeleton.[3]

```
1 public String front3(String str) {
2 // your code here
3 }
```

Listing 61: *front3 – skeleton*

Tools

For this problem you can use conditional statements, comparison operators, string concatenation as well as the string methods `length` and `substring`.

Hints

This is a very straight-forward problem, which you should be able to solve right away. As it does not contain any concepts you have not encountered so far, I would recommend that you revisit the preceding string problems if you get stuck.

---

[3]This is another string problem that should have placed earlier in the Warmup-1 sequence as it is conceptually simpler than the preceding one.

Solution

We will develop a more elegant solution in a short while, but a correct and perfectly adequate one is given below in Listing 62.

```
1 public String front3(String str) {
2   if (str.length() <= 3) {
3     return str + str + str;
4   } else {
5     String front = str.substring(0, 3);
6     return front + front + front;
7   }
8 }
```

Listing 62: front3 – solution

Discussion

The solution given above in Listing 62 is fine, but let us look at an alternative. We start by checking whether the length of the string is less than 3 and adjusting the value of front accordingly. The code is given in Listing 63 below.

```
1 public String front3(String str) {
2   String front;
3   if (str.length() < 3) {
4     front = str;
5   } else {
6     front = str.substring(0, 3);
7   }
8   return front + front + front;
9 }
```

Listing 63: front3 – variation 1

Do you see how the code in Listing 63 could be further simplified? If not, think of how to use the ternary operator in this case. The resulting code is given in Listing 64.

```
1 public String front3(String str) {
2   String front =
3     (str.length() < 3) ? str : str.substring(0, 3);
4   return front + front + front;
5 }
```

Listing 64: front3 – variation 2

Alternatively, you could dynamically adjust the second argument of the `substring` method as in Listing 65. This is a relatively advanced approach of solving such problems that would be non-obvious to plenty of programmers.

```java
public String front3(String str) {
    int    end   = str.length() <= 3 ? str.length() : 3;
    String front = str.substring(0, end);
    return front + front + front;
}
```

Listing 65: *front3 – variation 3*

backAround

Problem

The function `backAround` takes a string `str` as its input. The output is a string that has the last character of `str` prepended and appended, i.e. added to the front as well as the back. The string `str` is at least of length 1. See Listing 66 for the code skeleton.

```
1 public String backAround(String str) {
2 // your code here
3 }
```

Listing 66: backAround − skeleton

Tools

For this problem you will need to use the string concatenation operator and the string methods `length` as well as `charAt`.

Hints

This should be a very easy problem. If you are stuck, think about how you can use the string method `length` to extract the last character of a string.

Solution

This is as straightforward as it gets. Take the last character of the input string `str` and append as well as prepend it to `str`. Listing 67 has the solution.

```
1  public String backAround(String str) {
2    char last = str.charAt(str.length() - 1);
3    return last + str + last;
4  }
```

Listing 67: `backAround` – solution

Discussion

We start by determining the position of the last character of the input string `str`. Since we count from 0 upward, the position of that character is given by `str.length() - 1`. Afterwards, use that positional value to extract the character at that position from `str`. See Listing 68 for the corresponding code. Of course, you can as well condense lines 2 and 3 into one line, which I have done in Listing 67 above.

```
1  public String backAround(String str) {
2    int  last     = str.length() - 1;
3    char lastChar = str.charAt(last);
4    return lastChar + str + lastChar;
5  }
```

Listing 68: `backAround` – variation

or35

Problem

In or35 you get introduced to the modulo operator. The function you are asked to write takes an integer n as input and returns true if n is a multiple of 3 or if n is a multiple of 5. Otherwise, return false. Refer to Listing 69 for the code skeleton.

```
1 public boolean or35(int n) {
2 // your code here
3 }
```

Listing 69: or35 – skeleton

Tools

Tools you can use include conditional statements, boolean operators, the equality operator as well as the modulo operator.

Hints

For this problem you do not need to know how the modulo operator (%) works. Viewing it as a blackbox that computes the remainder when dividing n by m is sufficient. Of course, it cannot hurt to know about modulo arithmetic. In short, m % n returns m if it is the case that m < n. Otherwise, the modulo operator computes (m - n) % n. As you can see, you subtract n repeatedly, until the resulting number is less than n. Keep in mind that n can neither be negative nor zero.

Solution

First we check whether the remainder of n % 3 is equal to zero. Afterwards, we check whether the remainder of n % 5 is equal to zero. Finally, we combine both conditions with the disjunction operator for brevity. Refer to Listing 70 for the code.

```
1 public boolean or35(int n) {
2   return (n % 3 == 0) || (n % 5 == 0);
3 }
```

Listing 70: or35 – solution

front22

Problem

The problem front22 is a variation of the previously discussed problem front3. It takes a string str as input and returns str with the first two characters of str added to the front and back. If str is less than two characters long, then add the entire string to the front and back. Refer to Listing 71 for the code skeleton.

```
1 public String front22(String str) {
2 // your code here
3 }
```

Listing 71: front22 – skeleton

Tools

For this problem, use conditional statements, comparisons, the string concatenation operator as well as the string methods length and substring.

Hints

Since this problem is very similar to front3, you may want to use that problem as the foundation of your solution.

Solution

The solution in Listing 72 below is based on variation 2 of the solution to the previously discussed problem front3, which is repeated in Listing 73.

```
1  public String front22(String str) {
2    String front =
3      (str.length() < 2) ? str : str.substring(0, 2);
4    return front + str + front;
5  }
```

Listing 72: front22 – solution

Discussion

In this problem, we will encounter a fairly common task in professional software development, namely adapting a similar existing piece of code. We already have a solution to a very similar problem. In Listing 73 below, it is reproduced. As you can see, we produce a string that is a concatenation of three copies of front.

```
1  public String front3(String str) {
2    String front =
3      (str.length() < 3) ? str : str.substring(0, 3);
4    return front + front + front;
5  }
```

Listing 73: front3 – variation 2

Now, look at the code and see how you can quickly adapt it for the problem front22. You have to change the function name, replace the integer 3 with the integer 2 in line 3, and finally modify the return statement. The resulting solution is reproduced in Listing 74. The main takeaway is that it can be much faster to modify an existing piece of code than writing code from scratch. Of course, in this case producing the solution from scratch should not have been too difficult either.

```
1  public String front22(String str) {
2    String front =
3      (str.length() < 2) ? str : str.substring(0, 2);
4    return front + str + front;
5  }
```

Listing 74: front22 – solution

startHi

Problem

The aim of the functionf `startHi` is to return `true` if the provided string `str` starts with `"Hi"`. Otherwise, return `false`. Refer to Listing 75 for the code skeleton.

```
1 public boolean startHi(String str) {
2 // your code here
3 }
```

Listing 75: *startHi – skeleton*

Tools

For this problem, you can use conditional statements, boolean operators, and comparison operators. In addition, you will have to use the string methods `length`, `substring`, and `equals`.

Hints

A string of length less than 2 cannot possibly start with `"Hi"`. Thus, you need to take this case into account.

Solution

The solution provided below in Listing 76 directly follows the problem description. If the string is of a length less than 2, we return `false`. Otherwise, we check if the first two letters of the provided string `str` are equal to "Hi". We will see a different approach in the subsequent discussion.

```
1 public boolean startHi(String str) {
2   if (str.length() < 2) {
3     return false;
4   }
5   return str.substring(0, 2).equals("hi");
6 }
```

Listing 76: startHi – solution

Discussion

The solution provided in Listing 76 is perfectly adequate, but there is a different approach. Let us say you started with a more verbose solution, like the one in Listing 77 below. The order of the if-statements is fixed because checking for the substring requires that the string is at least of the indicated length. Otherwise, Java will throw an exception.

```
1 public boolean startHi(String str) {
2   if (str.length() < 2) {
3     return false;
4   }
5   if (str.substring(0, 2).equals("hi")) {
6     return true;
7   }
8   return false;
9 }
```

Listing 77: startHi – variation

Let us now reformulate the first condition so that it returns `true` as well, while producing the same result as the existing conditional statement. In order to do so, you need to flip both the comparison operator of the first if-statement and the boolean value of the associated return value. The code is shown in Listing 78.

```
1 public boolean startHi(String str) {
2   if (str.length() >= 2) {
3     return true;
4   }
5   if (str.substring(0, 2).equals("hi")) {
6     return true;
7   }
8   return false;
9 }
```

Listing 78: startHi – variation 2 (incomplete)

That was not right, unfortunately. Of course, we now need to nest the second if-statement because we otherwise wrongly indicate that every string that is at least of length 2 meets the provided criterion. The code is presented in Listing 79, which shows the finalized version of variation 2 of our solution. Look at the code and see if you can find a way to further simplify it.

```
1 public boolean startHi(String str) {
2   if (str.length() >= 2) {
3     if (str.substring(0, 2).equals("hi")) {
4       return true;
5     }
6   }
7   return false;
8 }
```

Listing 79: startHi – variation 2

The nested if-statement seen in the code in Listing 79 can be removed. If the condition we check is true, we return `true`. Otherwise, the execution path leaves both if-statements, the outer and the inner one, and we return `false`. Note that the inner if-statement is missing a case for returning `false` because that is the default return value of that function anyway, so there is no need to specify that return value twice. To clean up the code, we return the result of the condition in the nested if-clause. Refer to the code in Listing 80. I would stop at that point as that solution is very readable. We will look at an even more concise version in a moment, though.

```
1 public boolean startHi(String str) {
2   if (str.length() >= 2) {
3     return str.substring(0, 2).equals("hi");
4   }
5   return false;
6 }
```

Listing 80: startHi – variation 3

We can simplify this even further and eliminate the conditional statement altogether. This is only possible because Java uses so-called *short-circuit evaluation* for boolean operators. In this case, this means that if the first check returns `false`, the entire result is false anyway, thus there is no need to verify the second statement. See Listing 81 for the code. This is a somewhat obscure approach. It is interesting to know of it, but you may not want to use it much in practice.

```
1 public boolean startHi(String str) {
2   return (str.length() >= 2)
3         && str.substring(0,2).equals("hi");
4 }
```

Listing 81: startHi – variation 4

icyHot

Problem

The function `icyHot` takes two integers `temp1` and `temp2` as input. It returns `true` if one of the provided values is less than 0, and the other greater than 100. Refer to Listing 82 for the code skeleton.

```
1 public boolean icyHot(int temp1, int temp2) {
2 // your code here
3 }
```

Listing 82: icyHot – skeleton

Tools

For this problem, you can use conditional statements, comparison operators, and boolean operators.

Hints

Think about what the possible combinations are. Check whether the desired combinations are fulfilled. If so, return `true`. Otherwise, return `false`.

Solution

We will start with a straightforward solution, provided in Listing 83. Afterwards, we will transform it into a more elegant one.

```java
public boolean icyHot(int temp1, int temp2) {
  if (temp1 < 0 && temp2 > 100) {
    return true;
  }
  if (temp1 > 100 && temp2 < 0) {
    return true;
  }
  return false;
}
```

Listing 83: icyHot – solution

Discussion

The solution provided in Listing 83 is as straightforward as it gets as it directly translates the requirements into code. As you can see from that code, though, it is not the most concise solution. One could of course shorten it a little bit by joining both if-clauses, as in Listing 84.

```java
public boolean icyHot(int temp1, int temp2) {
  if ((temp1 < 0 && temp2 > 100)
    || (temp1 > 100 && temp2 < 0)) {
    return true;
  }
  return false;
}
```

Listing 84: icyHot – variation 1

You have seen similar patterns as in the code in Listing 84 before. Now, we can completely drop the if-statement and turn the code into a one-liner as in Listing 85, due to the fact that an if-statement of that form is redundant. We can as well just return the condition right away.

```
1 public boolean icyHot(int temp1, int temp2) {
2    return (temp1 < 0 && temp2 > 100)
3          || (temp1 > 100 && temp2 < 0);
4 }
```

Listing 85: icyHot – variation 2

This problem also points towards a common issue in software development: incomplete test coverage. The tests on Coding Bat omit the case where one number is less than -100, while the other is positive. You may think that is is an odd case. However, you can pass this problem with an alternative solution that may strike you as very elegant. Let us say you take a step back and think about the input. You wonder if there is a way to perform a simple operation that could determine whether one of the provided numbers is below 0, and the other above 100? Maybe think of the range of integers the product of both numbers has to be in. Think about it for a little bit.

Well, there is such a way. Listing 86 has the answer: if the product of both integers temp1 and temp2 is less than 100, then one of them is below 0, and the other above 100. As elegant as this may be, it is sadly incorrect as this approach does not exclude some illegal cases. This solution passes all test cases, even though it should not as it does not conform to the problem specification. Consider this example: temp1 equals -100, and temp2 equals 2. Their product is -200, which is obviously less than -100. Consequently, the return value is true. However, this case should return false, according to the problem statement, as one value is less than 0, but the other one is not greater than 100. You may think this discussion is superfluous, but in professional software development, accurately specifying what the code is supposed to do is not a trivial task, and neither is writing test cases that capture the specification. In our case, Listing 86 should not be correct, but because the test cases on Coding Bat are not sufficient for this example, at the time of writing, it is seen as correct.[4]

---

[4]The test cases on Coding Bat are, including the expected return value: 120 and -1 (true), -1 and 120 (true), 2 and 120 (false), -1 and 100 (false), -2 and -2 (false), 120 and 120 (false). A case like -100 and 2 (false) is unfortunately missing.

```
1 public boolean icyHot(int temp1, int temp2) {
2   return temp1 * temp2 < -100;
3 }
```

Listing 86: icyHot – variation 3 (incorrect)

Even if the code in Listing 86 were correct, a potential downside of it is that we only indirectly encode the specification of the problem as we went from considering two conditions to manipulating the input values and checking for a particular combined property.

in1020

Problem

The function in1020 takes two integers a, b as input and returns true if one of them is in the range [10 . . . 20]. Otherwise, it returns false. See Listing 87 for the code skeleton.

```
1 public boolean in1020(int a, int b) {
2 // your code here
3 }
```

Listing 87: in1020 – skeleton

Tools

For this problem you can use conditional statements, comparison operators, and boolean operators.

Hints

This is very straightforward. As a start, tackle both cases in turn, i.e. you first check a, followed by b and determine if they are in the prescribed range of integers.

Solution

The code in Listing 88 shows a straightforward solution. In the subsequent discussion, we will see a more elegant approach, though.

```
1  public boolean in1020(int a, int b) {
2    return (a >= 10 && a <= 20) || (b >= 10 && b <= 20);
3  }
```

Listing 88: in1020 – solution

Discussion

Let us start by checking both integers in separate if-statements. As you can see in the code shown in Listing 89, there is quite some duplication. We perform the exact same check, on different values, twice. This does not change if we rewrite the code into a more concise form, like in Listing 88 above.

```
1  public boolean in1020(int a, int b) {
2    if (a >= 10 && a <= 20) {
3      return true;
4    }
5    if (b >= 10 && b <= 20) {
6      return true;
7    }
8    return false;
9  }
```

Listing 89: in1020 – variation 1

Indeed, a downside of this exercise is that it teaches you to duplicate code, which is a rather bad habit to acquire. If you encountered a problem like this in the real world, you would instead create a separate helper function. This is goes a bit beyond what Coding Bat teaches up to this point, so view the code given in Listing 90 as a reference. As you can see, the helper function inRange checks whether the argument n is within the desired range. Thus, we replace the actual computation shown in Listing 88 with two function calls.

```
1 public boolean in1020(int a, int b) {
2   return inRange(a) || inRange(b);
3 }
4
5 public boolean inRange(int n) {
6   return n >= 10 && n <= 20;
7 }
```

Listing 90: *in1020* – variation 2

hasTeen

Problem

The function hasTeen takes three integers a, b, and c as inputs
and indicates if at least one of them is in the range [13 ... 19].
This problem is very similar to the preceding one, in1020. The
code skeleton is given in Listing 91.

```
1 public boolean hasTeen(int a, int b, int c) {
2 // your code here
3 }
```

Listing 91: *hasTeen – skeleton*

Tools

For this problem you can use conditional statements, comparison
operators, and boolean operators.

Hints

To keep this problem as simple as it is, consider that you can
use boolean operators sequentially. This means that if you want
to, for instance, check whether one of the three conditions c1,
c2, and c3 is true, you can write c1 || c2 || c3.

Solution

For each integer a, b, c we check if it is in the desired range. These checks can be performed with a sequence of or-statements. The code is given in Listing 92.

```
1 public boolean hasTeen(int a, int b, int c) {
2   return (a >= 13 && a <= 19)
3        || (b >= 13 && b <= 19)
4        || (c >= 13 && c <= 19);
5 }
```

Listing 92: hasTeen – solution

Discussion

This problem is very similar to the previous one, in1020. You may not like seeing three conditional checks in one statement, though. A less direct way of formulating a solution, which I would recommend in the case of more complicated checks, is thus given in Listing 93.

```
1 public boolean hasTeen(int a, int b, int c) {
2   boolean check_a = a >= 13 && a <= 19;
3   boolean check_b = b >= 13 && b <= 19;
4   boolean check_c = c >= 13 && c <= 19;
5   return check_a || check_b || check_c;
6 }
```

Listing 93: hasTeen – variation 1

Due to code duplication, you may want to use a separate helper function, as shown in Listing 94

```
1 public boolean hasTeen(int a, int b, int c) {
2   boolean check_a = inRange(a);
3   boolean check_b = inRange(b);
4   boolean check_c = inRange(c);
5   return check_a || check_b || check_c;
6 }
7
8 public boolean inRange(int n) {
9   return n >= 13 && n <= 19;
10 }
```

Listing 94: hasTeen – variation 2

At this point, you will see that we can just as well rewrite the function hasTeen to make it more readable. After all, defining three separate boolean variables is now clearly superfluous as they simply store the return value of a function call to inRange. The code is shown in Listing 95.

```java
1 public boolean hasTeen(int a, int b, int c) {
2   return inRange(a) || inRange(b) || inRange(c);
3 }
4
5 public boolean inRange(int n) {
6   return n >= 13 && n <= 19;
7 }
```

Listing 95: hasTeen – variation 3

loneTeen

Problem

The function loneTeen takes two integers as arguments. The goal is to determine if exactly one of them is in the range [13 ... 19]. This problem is a variation of the problem in1020. Refer to Listing 96 for the code skeleton.

```
1 public boolean loneTeen(int a, int b) {
2 // your code here
3 }
```

Listing 96: loneTeen – skeleton

Tools

For this problem you can use conditional statements, comparison operators, and boolean operators.

Hints

While in in1020 the goal was to find out whether at least one of the numbers is in a particular range, the goal of loneTeen is to check that this is true for exactly one number. Thus, you have to check that one number fulfills the condition, while the other does not.

Solution

The solution in Listing 97 is similar to the solutions of the previous problems. The helper function inRange is used to make the code more concise.

```
1  public boolean loneTeen(int a, int b) {
2    return inRange(a) && !inRange(b)
3           || !inRange(a) && inRange(b);
4  }
5
6  public boolean inRange(int n) {
7    return n >= 13 && n <= 19;
8  }
```

Listing 97: loneTeen – solution

Discussion

You need to express in code that exactly one of two conditions is true. This means that it has to be the case that, of two conditions a and b, it is the case that a && !b or !a && b. Using a helper function, you end up with the code shown in Listing 97 above. However, Java also knows an operator to express that exactly one of two cases is true, namely the *either-or*-operator, also referred to as *xor*-operator, which is expressed with the caret symbol (^). This allows us to express the previous solution more succinctly. See Listing 98 for the code. The xor-operator is not used much in practice. In fact, you will encounter it very rarely in real-world code. Consequently, it may be better to avoid it.

```
1  public boolean loneTeen(int a, int b) {
2    return inRange(a) ^ inRange(b);
3  }
4
5  public boolean inRange(int n) {
6    return n >= 13 && n <= 19;
7  }
```

Listing 98: loneTeen – variation 1

If you feel uncomfortable with helper functions, you can of course remove it and turn the solution into a one-line statement as in Listing 99.

81

```
1  public boolean loneTeen(int a, int b) {
2    return (a >= 13 & a <= 19) ^ (b >= 13 && b <= 19);
3  }
```

Listing 99: loneTeen – variation 2

delDel

Problem

The function delDel takes as its input a string str. If this string contains the substring "del", starting at position 1, then return a string with this substring removed. Otherwise, return str. The code skeleton is given in Listing 100.

```
1  public String delDel(String str) {
2  // your code here
3  }
```

Listing 100: delDel – skeleton

Tools

For this problem, you are free to use conditional statements, comparison operators, the string concatenation operator and the following string methods: length, substring, equals, and charAt.

Hints

You have to take into account cases where the input string is not at least 4 characters long. Once you have taken this case into account, use the string methods mentioned above.

Solution

We first check that the input string is at least 4 characters long. Afterwards, we check for equality as specified above, and return the modified string if needed. Refer to Listing 101 for the code.

```java
public String delDel(String str) {
  if (str.length() > 3) {
    if (str.substring(1, 4).equals("del")) {
      return str.charAt(0) + str.substring(4);
    }
  }
  return str;
}
```

Listing 101: delDel – solution

Discussion

Due to Java evaluating boolean expressions one-by-one, it is possible to combine the length check and the comparison with a substring of the input in one if-clause. If the entire condition in the if-clause evaluates to true, we return a modified string. Otherwise, the input string str is returned unchanged. The solution is very similar to previous problems, so it does not seem necessary to do a very detailed discussion. There is one aspect I would like to draw attention to, however. Look at the alternative solution presented in Listing 102. This is based on the idea of simply combining both if-statements from Listing 101 into one. It is also a valid solution. Yet, it is a matter of taste which one to prefer. In my opinion, a nested if-statement is preferable to a long singe if-statement with multiple conditions.

```java
public String delDel(String str) {
  if ((str.length() > 3)
      && (str.substring(1, 4).equals("del"))) {
    return str.charAt(0) + str.substring(4);
  }
  return str;
}
```

Listing 102: delDel – variation

mixStart

Problem

The problem `mixStart` determines whether the second and third letter of the input string `str` are equal to `"ix"`. This is another one of a small number of problems on Coding Bat, which would arguably fit better at an earlier point in the sequence of problems. The skeleton of the problem is given in Listing 103.

```
1 public boolean mixStart(String str) {
2 // your code here
3 }
```

Listing 103: mixStart – skeleton

Tools

For this problem you can use conditional statements, boolean operators, and the following string methods: `length`, `substring`, and `equals`.

Hints

This problem is very similar to the previous one. If you are stuck, revisit the problem `delDel`.

Solution

As the problem description indicates, we need to first check whether the provided string `str` is at least of length 3, before we can check that the second and third letter are equal to `"ix"`. See Listing 104 for the solution.

```
1 public boolean mixStart(String str) {
2   return str.length() >= 3
3         && str.substring(1, 3).equals("ix");
4 }
```

Listing 104: mixStart – solution

Discussion

This problem is essentially contained in the problem `delDel`. A separate discussion therefore seems unnecessary.

startOz

Problem

The function startOz takes a string str as input. The goal is to retain the first letter only if it is equal to 'o' and the second letter only if it is equal to 'z'. The code skeleton is given in Listing 105 below.

```
1 public String startOz(String str) {
2 // your code here
3 }
```

Listing 105: startOz – skeleton

Tools

For this problem you can use conditional statements, comparison operators, and boolean operators. You will also have to use the string concatenation operator. In addition, you will need the string methods length and charAt.

Hints

This problem introduces a very common pattern for handling string problems, namely using an accumulator. Define a variable holding an empty string and add to it as necessary.

Solution

We start with an accumulator variable `acc` and add to it as needed. The expression `str += x` is equivalent to `str = str + x`. See Listing 106 for the code.

```
1 public String startOz(String str) {
2   String acc = "";
3   if (str.length() > 0 && str.charAt(0) == 'o') acc += 'o';
4   if (str.length() > 1 && str.charAt(1) == 'z') acc += 'z';
5   return acc;
6 }
```

Listing 106: startOz – solution

Discussion

When starting out, the first thing to do is initializing an accumulator variable `acc`. As the default value to return is the empty string, this is precisely what we initialize the variable `acc` to. Afterwards, add if-statements that check whether the input string `str` is greater than zero as well as greater than one. For each clause, the next step is to add a letter to the accumulator based on the conditions laid out in the problem description. Listing 107 shows the code.

```
1  public String startOz(String str) {
2    String acc = "";
3    if (str.length() > 0 && str.charAt(0) == 'o') {
4      acc = acc + 'o';
5    }
6    if (str.length() > 1 && str.charAt(1) == 'z') {
7      acc = acc + 'z';
8    }
9    return acc;
10 }
```

Listing 107: startOz – variation 1

This is a perfectly fine solution. However, there is a shorthand for assigning to a string and concatenating it with another string or character. This can be done with the symbol += instead of repeating the name of the variable. With code this short, you can be excused for writing the complete if-statement on one line, as in Listing 108. You can even drop the curly braces, as shown in Listing 106. This example is one of the situations where it would be fine to do so, due to the fact that the code is quite simple. To be on the safe side for now, though, let us keep the curly braces.

```
1 public String startOz(String str) {
2   String acc = "";
3   if (str.length() > 0 && str.charAt(0) == 'o') {acc += 'o';}
4   if (str.length() > 1 && str.charAt(1) == 'z') {acc += 'z';}
5   return acc;
6 }
```

Listing 108: startOz – variation 2

intMax

Problem

The function `intMax` takes three integers a, b, and c as its input. Return the maximum of those three values. See Listing 109 for the code skeleton.

```
1 public int intMax(int a, int b, int c) {
2 // your code here
3 }
```

Listing 109: intMax skeleton

Tools

You can use conditional statements and comparison operators. However, you should not use the in-built method `Math.max`.

Hints

In order to determine the maximum of two numbers, first determine the maximum of two of those three numbers.

Solution

We start by assigning the first input value to the variable `max` and afterwards update it if necessary. The code is given in Listing 110.

```
1  public int intMax(int a, int b, int c) {
2      int max = a;
3      if (b > max) max = b;
4      if (c > max) max = c;
5      return max;
6  }
```

Listing 110: intMax – solution

Discussion

If you do not know that you can declare a variable without initializing it, you may feel stuck right away. Using that approach, you would first declare a variable `max` and afterwards assign the maximum of two out of the provided three numbers to it. However, we know that one of the three values has to be the maximum of the three provided integers, so instead of only declaring `max` and assigning a value to it after one comparison, we can just as well initially assign any of the input values to it. Afterwards we perform two checks and update the variable `max` as needed. The code is given in Listing 111.

```
1  public int intMax(int a, int b, int c) {
2    int max = a;
3    if (b > max) {
4      max = b;
5    }
6    if (c > max) {
7      max = c;
8    }
9    return max;
10 }
```

Listing 111: intMax – variation 1

With code this short, you can as well write the if-statements on a single line, like in Listing 110. For the sake of completeness, using the inbuilt method `Math.max` is illustrated in Listing 112.

```
1  public int intMax(int a, int b, int c) {
2    return Math.max(a, Math.max(b, c));
3  }
```

Listing 112: intMax – variation 2

close10

Problem

The function `close10` takes two integers `a` and `b` as input. Determine which of those integers is closer to 10 and return that value. Return 0 if there is no difference. The code skeleton is given in Listing 113.

```
1 public int close10(int a, int b) {
2 // your code here
3 }
```

Listing 113: close10 – skeleton

Tools

You can use conditional statements, comparison operators and the inbuilt method `Math.abs`. You will also have to use arithmetic operators.

Hints

There are only three possible cases. Tackle them one by one.

Solution

The solution in Listing 114 tackles the three possible cases sequentially. The code is very readable as it is, so the minimal amount of repetition does not pose a problem. In the discussion section, we will approach this problem slightly differently.

```
1 public int close10(int a, int b) {
2    if (Math.abs(10 - a) == Math.abs(10 - b)) return 0;
3    if (Math.abs(10 - a) <  Math.abs(10 - b)) return a;
4    return b;
5 }
```

Listing 114: close10 – solution

Discussion

We start by computing the absolute difference a and 10, followed by the absolute difference of b and 10. Afterwards, we perform comparisons as needed. You may feel tempted to encode a check for equality, like in Listing 115. There is a possibly more elegant way of solving this problem, however.

```
1 public int close10(int a, int b) {
2    int dist_a = Math.abs(a - 10);
3    int dist_b = Math.abs(b - 10);
4    if (dist_a == dist_b) {
5       return 0;
6    }
7    if (dist_a < dist_b) {
8       return a;
9    } else {
10      return b;
11   }
12 }
```

Listing 115: close10 – variation 1

Recall that there are only three possibilities. First, dist_a is the largest value. Second, dist_b is the largest value. Third, dist_a is identical to dist_b. What do we know if the first two conditions are not true? Then we know that both variables have to be equal. The code in Listing 116 uses this insight and consequently gets rid of the check for equality.

97

```
1  public int close10(int a, int b) {
2    int dist_a = Math.abs(a - 10);
3    int dist_b = Math.abs(b - 10);
4    if (dist_a < dist_b) {
5      return a;
6    } else if (dist_a > dist_b) {
7      return b;
8    } else {
9      return 0;
10   }
11 }
```

Listing 116: close10 – variation 2

Looking at the code in Listing 116, you may think that it is a lot more convoluted than it has to be. Sure, the final else-clause could be dropped and replaced by the associated return statement, but that is not the main issue. Instead, try keeping the check for equality and see if you can come up with a more elegant solution. In this case, the ternary operator could be used effectively. Before peeking ahead, try to find an alternative solution on your own. Afterwards, compare your solution with the one given in Listing 117.

The key aspect of that solution is that after taking care of the case where both differences are equal, we tackle the remaining two cases. Furthermore, we know that if diff_a is not less than diff_b, then it has to be the case that diff_b is greater than diff_a.

```
1  public int close10(int a, int b) {
2    int diff_a = Math.abs(10 - a);
3    int diff_b = Math.abs(10 - b);
4    if (diff_a == diff_b) return 0;
5    return (diff_a < diff_b) ? a : b;
6  }
```

Listing 117: close10 – variation 3

in3050

Problem

The problem in3050 is a repetition of concepts you have seen already. The goal is to write a function that takes two integers a and b as arguments and returns if they are both either in the range [30 ... 40] or in the range [40 ... 50]. The skeleton is given in Listing 118.

```
1 public boolean in3050(int a, int b) {
2 // your code here
3 }
```

Listing 118: in3050 – skeleton

Tools

You can use conditional statements, boolean operators and comparison operators.

Hints

Formulate two conditions and check whether at least one of them has been fulfilled.

Solution

We will start with a straightforward solution that contains some repetition. See Listing 119 below. In the discussion, we will refine it. Also, note that the parentheses are superfluous, but they make the code a lot more readable as you can immediately relate it to the conditions laid out in the problem statement.

```
1 public boolean in3050(int a, int b) {
2   boolean c1 = (a >= 30 && a <= 40) && (b >= 30 && b <= 40);
3   boolean c2 = (a >= 40 && a <= 50) && (b >= 40 && b <= 50);
4   return c1 || 2;
5 }
```

Listing 119: in3050 solution

Discussion

The solution shown in Listing 119 is perfectly adequate. However, there is quite some repetition, which can be removed to make the code a bit more elegant. If you remove the parentheses, however, it may take a bit longer to see how to simplify it. It would be even more obtuse if you rearranged the order of comparisons. Looking at the code as it is, though, it is quite obvious that you can factor out some computations. In Listing 120, we achieve this goal by defining two helper functions, inRange3040 and inRange4050.

```
1 public boolean in3050(int a, int b) {
2   boolean c1 = inRange3040(a) && inRange3040(b);
3   boolean c2 = inRange4050(a) && inRange4050(b);
4   return c1 || c2;
5 }
6
7 public boolean inRange3040(int x){
8   return x >= 30 && x <= 40;
9 }
10
11 public boolean inRange4050(int x){
12   return x >= 40 && x <= 50;
13 }
```

Listing 120: in3050 – variation 1

Do you see how this code could be simplified even further? I will give you a hint. What changes in the function body of the functions inRange3040 and inRange4050? Both functions are very similar. They only differ in the upper and lower limit of the range. So, let us factor this out as well. The resulting code is given in Listing 121.

```
1 public boolean in3050(int a, int b) {
2   boolean c1 = inRange(a, 30, 40) && inRange(b, 30, 40);
3   boolean c2 = inRange(a, 40, 50) && inRange(b, 40, 50);
4   return c1 || c2;
5 }
6
7 public boolean inRange(int x, int min, int max){
8   return x >= min && x <= max;
9 }
```

Listing 121: in3050 – variation 2

max1020

Problem

The function max1020 takes two integers a and b as input. Its goal is to return the larger of those two integers that is within the range [10 ... 20]. If none of them is in that range, return 0. The code skeleton is shown in Listing 122.

```
1 public int max1020(int a, int b) {
2 // your code here
3 }
```

Listing 122: max1020 – skeleton

Tools

You can use conditional statements, comparison operators, and boolean operators.

Hints

This can be a tricky problem. You could either list all possible cases of how the integers a and b relate to each other. Alternatively, you could make sure that a is never larger than b, and b never smaller than a.

Solution

To make his problem much more easily manageable, we swap the values of a and b, if necessary, so that a is always less than or equal to b. Afterwards, we determine whether any of those two variables is in the desired range. See Listing 123 for the code.

```
1  public int max1020(int a, int b) {
2    if (b < a) {
3      int temp = a;
4      a = b;
5      b = temp;
6    }
7    boolean aInRange = a >= 10 && a <= 20;
8    boolean bInRange = b >= 10 && b <= 20;
9    if (bInRange) return b;
10   if (aInRange) return a;
11   return 0;
12 }
```

Listing 123: max1020 – solution

Discussion

In order to solve this problem, you could either duplicate a large part of the code and take into account the two cases a >= b and a < b, like in the code shown in Listing 124. This is a fine solution. Yet, this problem can also be used to teach you a trick you may occasionally need as a programmer, namely swapping variables.

```
1  public int max1020(int a, int b) {
2    int res = 0;
3    if (a >= 10 && a <= 20) res = a;
4    if (b >= 10 && b <= 20) {
5      if (b > res) res = b;
6    }
7    return res;
8  }
```

Listing 124: max1020 – variation 1

In this problem, swapping variables is motivated by the fact that we would like to ensure that a is always smaller than or equal to b. Figuring out how to swap variables can be a bit tricky for a novice programmer as it is not necessarily obvious how to do so. In Java, you will have to use a temporary variable. Look at the code fragment in Listing 125. We want to swap a and b, but if we assigned the value of b to a right away, we would lose the value assigned to variable a. Thus, we need to temporarily store the value of a in a temporary variable temp. Afterwards, we assign the value of b to a. Once this is done, we retrieve the former value of a from the variable temp.

```
1  int temp = a;
2  a = b;
3  b = temp;
```

Listing 125: Swapping variables

Consequently, we can write up a more elegant solution to the original problem, which uses optional variable swapping and the helper function inRange to avoid code repetition. See Listing 126 for the code.

```
1  public int max1020(int a, int b) {
2    if (b > a) {
3      int temp = a;
4      a = b;
5      b = temp;
6    }
7    if (inRange(a)) return a;
8    if (inRange(b)) return b;
9    return 0;
10 }
11
12 public boolean inRange(int x) {
13   return x >= 10 && x <= 20;
14 }
```

Listing 126: max1020 – variation 2

stringE

Problem

The function `stringE` takes a string `str` as input and returns true if it contains the character `'e'` between 1 and 3 times. Otherwise, return `false`. The code skeleton is given in Listing 127.

```
1 public boolean stringE(String str) {
2 // your code here
3 }
```

Listing 127: stringE – skeleton

Tools

You can use conditional statements, comparison operators, a for-loop, arithmetic operators, and the string methods `length` as well as `charAt`.

Hints

Go through the input string `str` character by character and count how often you encounter the letter `'e'`. Afterwards, check if the number you have reached via counting is in the desired range.

Solution

The solution shown in Listing 128 shows a standard pattern of approaching such counting problems. You will see similar problems over and over, as loop are one of the main building blocks of computer programs.

```java
public boolean stringE(String str) {
  int count = 0;
  for (int i = 0; i < str.length(); i = i + 1) {
    if (str.charAt(i) == 'e') {
      count = count + 1;
    }
  }
  return count >= 1 && count <= 3;
}
```

Listing 128: stringE – solution

Discussion

This problem introduces you to for-loops, but does not pose any other difficulty. If you have read up on that concept, you should have little difficulty. First, we declare and initialize a variable count to 0. This variable is used for keeping track of the number of times we detect the character 'e' in the input string. The for-loop iterates through the entire string, and we compare each character of it with the character 'e'. Adding 1 to a number is so common that there is a shorthand for it in Java and many other programming languages, the ++ operator. We use it to shorten the body of the for-loop in the variation of the solution, which is given in Listing 129.

```java
public boolean stringE(String str) {
  int count = 0;
  for (int i = 0; i < str.length(); i++) {
    if (str.charAt(i) == 'e') count++;
  }
  return count >= 1 && count <= 3;
}
```

Listing 129: stringE – variation

lastDigit

Problem

The function `lastDigit` takes two integers a and b as its input. Return `true` if they end in the same digit. Otherwise, return `false`. The code skeleton is given in Listing 130.

```
1 public boolean lastDigit(int a, int b) {
2 // your code here
3 }
```

Listing 130: `lastDigit` – skeleton

Tools

You are free to use conditional operators, arithmetic operators, and the modulo operator. The modulo operator (%) computes the remainder.

Hints

This is a very straightforward problem. If you are stuck, refer to problem or35, which is related. Also, think about how you can extract the last digit of a number with the modulo operator.

Solution

This is a very straightforward problem. Use % 10 on both integers to extract the rightmost digit and check the resulting values for equality. See Listing 131 for the code.

```
1  public boolean lastDigit(int a, int b) {
2    return a % 10 == b % 10;
3  }
```

Listing 131: lastDigit – solution

Discussion

There is not much to this problem. One possibly interesting variation is to get rid of one of the modulo operators by computing the absolute difference of a and b, like in the code in Listing 132. It does not make much of a difference for this problem. However, in practice it can be helpful to simplify the data you are working with before performing expensive operations.

```
1  public boolean lastDigit(int a, int b) {
2    return Math.abs(a - b) % 10 == 0;
3  }
```

Listing 132: lastDigit – variation

endUp

Problem

The function endUp takes a string str as input. If that string
is of length 3 or less, return the entire string in uppercase.
Otherwise, return a string that is identical to str, except that
the last three characters have been turned into uppercase. The
code skeleton is provided in Listing 133.

```
1 public String endUp(String str) {
2 // your code here
3 }
```

Listing 133: endUp – skeleton

Tools

For this problem you can use arithmetic operators, conditional
statements, the string concatenation operator and the following
string methods: substring, length, and toUpperCase.

Hints

Take care of the case where the input string is at most of length
3 first.

Solution

A concise but sub-optimal solution is given in Listing 134. We first take care of the possibility that the input string is less than 3 characters long. Afterwards, that is the case in which the input string is at least 3 characters long, we construct a new string where the last three characters have been turned into uppercase.

```
1 public String endUp(String str) {
2   if (str.length() < 3) return str.toUpperCase();
3   return str.substring(0, str.length() - 3)
4         + str.substring(str.length() - 3).toUpperCase();
5 }
```

Listing 134: endUp – solution

Discussion

We start by checking if the input string str is less than three characters long. If this is the case, we simply turn the entire input string into uppercase. Alternatively, we extract the last three characters, turn that substring into uppercase and construct the required output. This is shown in Listing 135.

```
1 public String endUp(String str) {
2   if (str.length() < 3) {
3     return str.toUpperCase();
4   }
5   String lastThree = str.substring(str.length() - 3);
6   lastThree       = lastThree.toUpperCase();
7   return str.substring(0, str.length() - 3) + lastThree;
8 }
```

Listing 135: endUp – variation 1

The solution you have just seen would be even more readable if we also named the part of the string we do not modify, like in Listing 136. The substring front consists of all characters except the last three, provided the input string str is at least of length 3. By using separate variables for naming intermediate results, the resulting code becomes a lot more readable.

```
1 public String endUp(String str) {
2   if (str.length() < 3) {
3     return str.toUpperCase();
4   }
5   String front = str.substring(0, str.length() - 3);
6   String back  = str.substring(str.length() - 3);
7   back          = back.toUpperCase();
8   return front + back;
9 }
```

Listing 136: endUp – variation 2

everyNth

Problem

The function everyNth takes a string str and an integer n as its input. Its output consists of a string made up of every n^{th} character of str. The code skeleton is shown in Listing 137.

```
1  public String everyNth(String str, int n) {
2  // your code here
3  }
```

Listing 137: everyNth – skeleton

Tools

You can use a for-loop, conditional expressions, the string concatenation operator, and the modulo operator. You will also have to use the string methods charAt and length.

Hints

A straightforward solution is to keep track of the position you are in the string, check if it is an nth position and if so, retain the character at that position.

116

Solution

Not the most elegant but certainly a valid approach is to set up a for-loop that iterates through every character and checks if the iterator variable i is at the nth position with the modulo operator. The code is shown in Listing 138.

```
1 public String everyNth(String str, int n) {
2   String result = "";
3   for (int i = 0; i < str.length(); i++) {
4     if (i % n == 0) {
5       result += str.charAt(i);
6     }
7   }
8   return result;
9 }
```

Listing 138: everyNth – solution

Discussion

There is an interesting twist to this problem. While a straight-forward approach is to iterate through the entire string and check whether the current position is an nth position, as shown in Listing 138, you may also use the for-loop to iterate through only every n^{th} position. This simplifies the code. The final result is shown in Listing 139

```
1 public String everyNth(String str, int n) {
2   String res = "";
3   for (int i = 0; i < str.length(); i += n) {
4     res += str.charAt(i);
5   }
6   return res;
7 }
```

Listing 139: everyNth – variation

String-1

helloName

Problem

The function `helloName` takes as its input a string name. The output consists of that string prepended with `"Hello "` and appended with `'!'`. The code skeleton is shown in Listing 140.

```
1  public String helloName(String name) {
2  // your code here
3  }
```

Listing 140: helloName – skeleton

Tools

You only need the string concatenation operator for this problem.

Hints

Keep in mind that you can use the string concatenation operator multiple times in a single statement.

Solution

This is a simple problem. All you need to do is construct a new string where the first part consists of the string "Hello ", the second part of the input string name, and the third part of either the string "!" or the character '!'. The code is shown in Listing 141.

```
1 public String helloName(String name) {
2   return "Hello " + name + '!';
3 }
```

Listing 141: helloName – solution

makeAbba

Problem

The function `makeAbba` takes two strings a and b as its input and produces a string that consists of a followed by b, followed by b, followed by a. The code skeleton is provided in Listing 142.

```
1 public String makeAbba(String a, String b) {
2 // your code here
3 }
```

Listing 142: makeAbba – skeleton

Tools

You only need to use the string concatenation operator for this problem.

Hints

This problem is very similar to the previous one.

Solution

This is one of the most trivial problems in the entire suite of problems on Coding Bat. All you need to do is concatenate the input strings as shown in Listing 143.

```
1 public String makeAbba(String a, String b) {
2    return a + b + b + a;
3 }
```

Listing 143: makeAbba − solution

makeTags

Problem

The function `makeTags` takes two strings `tag` and `word` as its input. The goal is to put `word` into an HTML tag `tag`. The format of an HTML tag is as follows. An opening tag is followed by some text, i.e. `word` in our example, which is followed by a closing tag. For instance, if the tag is called `sub`, the opening tag is `"<sub>"` and the closing tag `"</sub>"`. The code skeleton is given in Listing 144.

```
1 public String makeTags(String tag, String word) {
2 // your code here
3 }
```

Listing 144: makeTags – skeleton

Tools

For this problem you only need to use the string concatenation operator.

Hints

In case it is not obvious, you can hard-code the required symbols for creating an HTML tag.

Solution

As described earlier, we construct the opening and closing tags, and place the string word in between them. The code is shown in Listing 145.

```
1 public String makeTags(String tag, String word) {
2   return "<" + tag + ">" + word + "</" + tag + ">";
3 }
```

Listing 145: makeTags – solution

makeOutWord

Problem

The function makeOutWord takes two strings out and word as
its input. The string out is of length 4. The goal is to produce
a new string that consists of the first two characters of out,
followed by word, followed by the last two characters of out.
The code skeleton is given in Listing 146.

```
1 public String makeOutWord(String out, String word) {
2 // your code here
3 }
```

Listing 146: makeOutWord – skeleton

Tools

For this problem, you will have to use the string concatenation
operator as well as the string method substring.

Hints

Start by splitting the string out into two parts.

Solution

Use the string method `substring` to create two substrings, one containing the first two characters, and one containing the last two characters. Respectively prepend and append them to the string `word` as shown in Listing 147.

```java
public String makeOutWord(String out, String word) {
  return out.substring(0, 2) + word + out.substring(2);
}
```

Listing 147: makeOutWord – solution

extraEnd

Problem

The function extraEnd takes a string str as its input and returns a new string containing the last two characters of str three times in a row. The input string is at least of length 2. The code skeleton is given in Listing 148.

```
1 public String extraEnd(String str) {
2 // your code here
3 }
```

Listing 148: extraEnd – skeleton

Tools

You will need to use the string methods substring and length as well as the string concatenation operator.

Hints

Try to make your solution cleaner by storing the results of one particular computation in a separate variable. Furthermore, in order to extract the last two characters of the input string str, you will have to use the string method length in order to determine where the substring should start.

Solution

First, we extract the last two characters of the input string str and assign the value to the variable end. Afterwards, we construct a new string, consisting of three copies of end. The code is shown in Listing 149.

```java
public String extraEnd(String str) {
  String end = str.substring(str.length() - 2);
  return end + end + end;
}
```

Listing 149: extraEnd – solution

firstTwo

Problem

The function firstTwo takes a string str as its input. If str is at least of length 2, return the first two characters of str. Otherwise, return str. The code skeleton is given in Listing 150.

```
1 public String firstTwo(String str) {
2 // your code here
3 }
```

Listing 150: *firstTwo – skeleton*

Tools

For this problem you will need to use the string methods length and substring, a conditional operator and a comparison operator.

Hints

Start by checking whether the string is less than two characters long.

Solution

We first check if the input string str is less than two characters long. If that is the case, we return str. Otherwise, we return the first two characters of str. The code is given in Listing 151.

```
1 public String firstTwo(String str) {
2   if (str.length() < 2) {
3     return str;
4   }
5   return str.substring(0, 2);
6 }
```

Listing 151: firstTwo – solution

Discussion

The code provided in Listing 151 is straightforward and perfectly acceptable. However, it may be neater to use a conditional statement as part of the argument to substring, either directly or indirectly. In Listing 152, we use a variable len that dynamically computes the length of the input string.

```
1 public String firstTwo(String str) {
2   int len = (str.length() < 2) ? str.length() : 2;
3   return str.substring(0, len);
4 }
```

Listing 152: firstTwo – varation 1

A different approach is shown by the code in Listing 153. There, we use the variable len only to make the code a bit more readable by using it as a shorthand for str.length(). This is one of the situations where the ternary operator is perfectly adequate.

```
1 public String firstTwo(String str) {
2   int len = str.length();
3   return str.substring(0, (len < 2) ? len : 2);
4 }
```

Listing 153: firstTwo – variation 2

firstHalf

Problem

The function `firstHalf` takes a string `str` as its input and returns the first half of it. All input strings are of even length. See Listing 154 for the code skeleton.

```
1 public String firstHalf(String str) {
2 // your code here
3 }
```

Listing 154: firstHalf – skeleton

Tools

For this problem you will have to use the string methods `substring` and `length`. You will also need arithmetic operators.

Hints

Think about how you can determine half of the length of a string of even length.

Solution

We first determine the midpoint of the string and use it as the cutoff for the method substring. The code is shown in Listing 155. Of course, you could turn this into a one-liner by replacing mid in the return statement with the expression it stands for.

```
1 public String firstHalf(String str) {
2   int mid = str.length() / 2;
3   return str.substring(0, mid);
4 }
```

Listing 155: firstHalf – solution

withoutEnd

Problem

The function `withoutEnd` takes a string `str` as input that is at least of length 2. The goal is to remove the first and last character from `str`. The code skeleton is given in Listing 156.

```
1  public String withoutEnd(String str) {
2  // your code here
3  }
```

Listing 156: withoutEnd – skeleton

Tools

You will have to use the string methods `length` and `substring`.

Hints

Use the string method `length` to determine the position of the second-to-last character of the string and use this as an argument for the string method `substring`.

Solution

This is a simple one-liner. Use the string method `substring`, starting at position 1 and ending at the second-to-last character of the string. See Listing 157 for the code.

```
1 public String withoutEnd(String str) {
2   return str.substring(1, str.length() - 1);
3 }
```

Listing 157: withoutEnd – solution

comboString

Problem

The function comboString takes two strings a and b as its input, which do not necessarily have the same length. If string a is the longer string, return a new string consisting of the concatenation of b, followed by a, followed by b. Otherwise, return a new string that is the result of the concatenation of a, followed by b, followed by a. See Listing 158 for the code skeleton.

```
1 public String comboString(String a, String b) {
2 // your code here
3 }
```

Listing 158: comboString – skeleton

Tools

This problem requires the use of a conditional statement, comparison operators, the string concatenation operator, and the string method length.

Hints

Start by determining which string is longer.

Solution

After determining which string is longer, we know which combination of strings we have to return. See Listing 159 for the code.

```
1 public String comboString(String a, String b) {
2   if (a.length() > b.length()) {
3     return b + a + b;
4   }
5   return a + b + a;
6 }
```

Listing 159: comboString – solution

Discussion

While the solution presented in Listing 159 is fine, it can be shortened significantly from four lines to just one line by using the ternary operator. While you should show restraint when it comes to that operator, it is suitable for the current problem because the operations are quite short. See Listing 160 for the code.

```
1 public String comboString(String a, String b) {
2   return a.length() > b.length() ? b + a + b : a + b + a;
3 }
```

Listing 160: comboString – variation

nonStart

Problem

The function nonStart takes two strings a and b as its input. It produces a string as it output that consists of the concatenation of a and b, with the first character of each of the two input strings omitted. The code skeleton is provided in Listing 161.

```
1 public String nonStart(String a, String b) {
2 // your code here
3 }
```

Listing 161: nonStart – skeleton

Tools

For this problem you will need to use the string method substring as well as the string concatenation operator.

Hints

This problem should not provide much of a challenge as it combines operations you have used before.

Solution

With the string method `substring`, we extract a substring starting at character 1 from both a and b and concatenate the result. See Listing 162 for the code.

```
1 public String nonStart(String a, String b) {
2   return a.substring(1) + b.substring(1);
3 }
```

Listing 162: nonStart – solution

left2

Problem

The function `left2` takes a string `str` as its input, which has a length of at least 2. It returns a string that is the concatenation of the substring of `str` starting at the second character and a substring containing the first two characters. The code skeleton is given in Listing 163.

```
1 public String left2(String str) {
2 // your code here
3 }
```

Listing 163: left2 – skeleton

Tools

For this problem, you will have to use the string method `substring` and the string concatenation operator.

Hints

Revisit the problem `nonStart`, if you are stuck. It is very similar to the current problem.

Solution

We create a new string consisting of a substring of `str` starting at character 2. We also need to extract a substring of `str` that contains the first two characters. Afterwards, we concatenate those two substrings, as shown in Listing 164.

```java
1 public String left2(String str) {
2   return str.substring(2) + str.substring(0, 2);
3 }
```

Listing 164: left2 – solution

right2

Problem

The function right2 takes a string str as its input, which is at least of length 2. It returns a string that results from the concatenation of a substring of str that contains the last two characters of str and a substring of str containing all but the last two characters. The code skeleton is given in Listing 165.

```
1 public String right2(String str) {
2 // your code here
3 }
```

Listing 165: right2 – skeleton

Tools

For this problem, you will have to use the string methods length and substring as well as the string concatenation operator.

Hints

Use the string method length to determine the cutoff points of the substrings you need to extract from the string str.

Solution

We will need to know the length of the input string. After determining it, we extract the desired substrings. The first one starts two characters before the end of the string, the other ends two characters before the end of the string. The code is given in Listing 166. In order to make the code more readable, the variable l has been used to store the length of the string.

```java
public String right2(String str) {
    int l = str.length();
    return str.substring(l - 2) + str.substring(0, l - 2);
}
```

Listing 166: right2 – solution

theEnd

Problem

The function `theEnd` takes a string `str` as well as a boolean `front` as its input. Return a string containing the first character of `str` if `front` is true. Otherwise, return a string that contains all characters of `str` except the very last one. The code skeleton is given in Listing 167.

```
1 public String theEnd(String str, boolean front) {
2 // your code here
3 }
```

Listing 167: *theEnd – skeleton*

Tools

For this problem you will have to use a conditional statement as well as the string methods `length` and `substring`.

Hints

Start by checking whether the boolean value `front` is true.

Solution

We start by checking whether `front` is true. If so, we return a substring consisting of the first character of the input string `str`. Otherwise, we use the string method `length` to extract a substring that contains all characters of `str` up to the second-to-last one. The code is provided in Listing 168.

```java
public String theEnd(String str, boolean front) {
    if (front) {
        return str.substring(0, 1);
    }
    return str.substring(str.length() - 1);
}
```

Listing 168: theEnd – solution

withouEnd2

Problem

The function `withouEnd2` — no, this is not a typo — takes as its input a string `str`. The goal is to return a new string that drops both the first and last character of `str`. The input string can be empty. See Listing 169 for the code skeleton.

```
1 public String withouEnd2(String str) {
2 // your code here
3 }
```

Listing 169: withouEnd2 – skeleton

Tools

This problem requires a conditional statement, a comparison operator, as well as the two string methods `length` and `substring`.

Hints

What happens if the input is the empty string or a string containing just one character? Take care of that case first.

Solution

In order to avoid an out-of-bounds error, we need to separately deal with strings that are less than two characters long. If this is the case, we return the empty string. Otherwise, we extract a substring from the first character (if you start counting from 0, like Java does) or the second character (if you start counting from 1, like humans normally do) of the string str all the way up to the second-to-last character. The code is provided in Listing 170.

```java
public String withouEnd2(String str) {
  if (str.length() < 2) {
    return "";
  }
  return str.substring(1, str.length() - 1);
}
```

Listing 170: withouEnd2 – solution

middleTwo

Problem

The function `middleTwo` takes an even-length string `str` as its input, which is of length 2 or more. The goal is to return a string consisting of the middle two characters of `str`. See Listing 171 for the code skeleton.

```
1 public String middleTwo(String str) {
2 // your code here
3 }
```

Listing 171: middleTwo – skeleton

Tools

For this problem, you will need to use the string methods `length` and `substring` as well as arithmetic operators.

Hints

Start by determining the position of the middle character of the input string `str`. If you have not yet gotten comfortable with string indexing, this problem might require a few additional tries, but it is not difficult.

Solution

We first determine mid, the position of the character in the middle. This is the second character of the output string. In order to properly delimit the substring, we subtract 1 from mid for the lower limit, and add 1 to mid for the upper limit. The resulting code is given in Listing 172.

```
1 public String middleTwo(String str) {
2   int mid = str.length() / 2;
3   return str.substring(mid - 1, mid + 1);
4 }
```

Listing 172: middleTwo – solution

endsLy

Problem

The function endsLy takes a string str as its input. The goal is to determine whether the input string ends with the letters "ly". The code skeleton is provided in Listing 173.

```
1 public boolean endsLy(String str) {
2 // your code here
3 }
```

Listing 173: endsLy – skeleton

Tools

This problem requires the use of a conditional statement, a comparison operator, as well as the string methods length, substring, and equals.

Hints

As indicated above, you will have to use the string method equals to compare a substring of the input string str with the string "ly". The equality operator (==) is not suitable as it determines whether two objects point to the same memory location. Also, take into account the case that the input string may be less than two characters long.

Solution

For conciseness, we compute the length of the input string only once and store the result as the variable 1. Afterwards, we check the length of the string. If the string is at least of length 2, we compare its last two characters with "ly". The code is given in Listing 174.

```
1 public boolean endsLy(String str) {
2    int l = str.length();
3    if (l < 2) {
4      return false;
5    }
6    return str.substring(l - 2).equals("ly");
7 }
```

Listing 174: endsLy – solution

Discussion

You may also want to condense the last four lines of code into just one by using the ternary operator, as shown in Listing 175. Arguably, the ternary operator works well in this case, making the resulting code both more concise and more readable.

```
1 public boolean endsLy(String str) {
2    int l = str.length();
3    return l < 2 ? false : str.substring(l - 2).equals("ly");
4 }
```

Listing 175: endsLy – variation

nTwice

Problem

The function nTwice takes a string str as well as an integer n as its input. The goal is to produce a string consisting of the concatenation of the first n characters of str as well as the last n characters of str. The input string str is at least n characters long. The code skeleton is given in Listing 176.

```
1 public String nTwice(String str, int n) {
2 // your code here
3 }
```

Listing 176: nTwice – skeleton

Tools

This problem requires the use of the string methods substring and length as well as the string concatenation operator.

Hints

This is a very straightforward problem. Think about how to extract the first n characters. Afterwards, try to extract the last n characters.

Solution

We start by extracting the first n characters from the input string via the string method substring. Afterwards, we use the string method length to figure out from where onward in the string str we have to extract a substring that contains the last n characters of it. Finally, we concatenate both values. The code is given in Listing 177.

```
1 public String nTwice(String str, int n) {
2   return str.substring(0, n)
3         + str.substring(str.length() - n);
4 }
```

Listing 177: nTwice – solution

twoChar

Problem

The function twoChar takes a string str and an integer index as its input. The input string is at least of length 2. The goal is to extract a substring of length 2 from str, beginning at position index. If the input integer index makes it impossible to extract a string of length 2, return a string containing the first two characters of str. The code skeleton is given in Listing 178.

```
1 public String twoChar(String str, int index) {
2 // your code here
3 }
```

Listing 178: twoChar – skeleton

Tools

This problem requires the use of a conditional statement and the comparison operator. You may also find some use for boolean operators. Furthermore, you will have to use the string methods substring and length.

Hints

Think about which values of index make it impossible to extract a substring of length 2 from str, which starts at position index.

154

Solution

Let us start by shortening the variable name `index` to `i` as it is somewhat unsightly to see such a needlessly long variable name, when `i` is a standard variable name for indexing. The key insight for solving this problem is that any value for `i` that is below 0 or greater than the length of `str` minus 2 is unsuitable for indexing into `str`. In that case, we return the first two characters of the input string `str`. Otherwise, we index into `str` and return a substring consisting of two characters, starting at position `i` The code is given in Listing 179.

```
1 public String twoChar(String str, int i) {
2   if (i < 0 || i > str.length() - 2) {
3     return str.substring(0, 2);
4   }
5   return str.substring(i, i + 2);
6 }
```

Listing 179: twoChar – solution

middleThree

Problem

The function `middleThree` takes as its input a string `str` of odd length that is at least three characters long. The goal is to return the middle three characters of it. The code skeleton is provided in Listing 180.

```
1 public String middleThree(String str) {
2 // your code here
3 }
```

Listing 180: middleThree – skeleton

Tools

This problem requires the use of the string methods `length` and `substring` in addition to arithmetic operators.

Hints

The key to this problem is the string method `substring`. Start by determining the middle character of the input string `str`.

Solution

After determining the position of the middle character of the odd-length input string, mid, we know how to delimit the substring that contains the middle three characters. We need to start one position to the left of mid and take three characters, as shown in Listing 181.

```java
public String middleThree(String str) {
    int mid = str.length() / 2;
    return str.substring(mid - 1, mid + 2);
}
```

Listing 181: middleThree – solution

Discussion

As concise as the code in Listing 181 may be, it obfuscates a simplification. In this example you may scoff at it, but more elegant indexing pays off in any larger project. So, humor me and literally translate the requirement of looking three characters to the right, starting from the position mid. The result is shown in Listing 182.

```java
public String middleThree(String str) {
    int mid = str.length() / 2;
    return str.substring(mid - 1, (mid - 1) + 3);
}
```

Listing 182: middleThree – variation 1

Yes, I know that this looks silly. But look again! You certainly see that there is a repetition of code that disappears if the second argument to the string method substring is expressed as mid + 2. Thus, we can simplify our solution and arrive at a code snippet that directly expresses that we start one character to the left of the middle character of the input. See Listing 183 for the final solution.

```java
public String middleThree(String str) {
    int pos = (str.length() / 2) - 1;
    return str.substring(pos, pos + 3);
}
```

Listing 183: middleThree – variation 2

hasBad

Problem

The function hasBad takes a string str as its input. The goal is to determine whether the input string contains the substring "bad" within the first four characters. Keep in mind that the input string can have any length. You will find the code skeleton in Listing 184.

```
1 public boolean hasBad(String str) {
2 // your code here
3 }
```

Listing 184: hasBad – skeleton

Tools

For this problem, you will have to use conditional statements, comparison operators, and the following string methods: length, substring, and equals.

Hints

Do not get sidetracked by finding a concise solution that is not there. Due to out-of-bound errors, you will have to write two very similar conditional statements.

Solution

We need to consider three cases of the input string `str`. First, we check if `str` is at least three characters long. If so, we check whether the first three characters of it are equal to the string "bad". Afterwards, we repeat this for strings that are at least four characters long, but looking at the three-letter substring starting at position 1. If none of those two cases were true, the return value is `false`. See Listing 185 for the code.

```
1  public boolean hasBad(String str) {
2    if (str.length() >= 3) {
3      if (str.substring(0, 3).equals("bad")) {
4        return true;
5      }
6    }
7    if (str.length() >= 4) {
8      if (str.substring(1, 4).equals("bad")) {
9        return true;
10     }
11   }
12   return false;
13 }
```

Listing 185: hasBad – solution

Discussion

As you have seen, the solution to this problem is rather inelegant. We unfortunately have to make the case distinction shown in order to avoid out-of-bounds errors. However, you could try to write a helper function to make the code a bit more concise. Can you see how to do it? My solution is given in Listing 186. The helper removes the code duplication of the equality check of a substring of `str`. The only difference of those method calls are the arguments, as one check starts at position 0, and the other at position 1.

```
1  public boolean hasBad(String str) {
2    if (str.length() >= 3) {
3      if (helper(str, 0)) {
4        return true;
5      }
6    }
7    if (str.length() >= 4) {
8      if (helper(str, 1)) {
9        return true;
10     }
11   }
12   return false;
13 }
14
15 public boolean helper(String str, int pos) {
16   return (str.substring(pos, pos + 3).equals("bad"));
17 }
```

Listing 186: hasBad – variation 1

But wait, we are not done yet! Let us use an accumulator variable `result`, initialized to `false`. If any of the conditions is true, we set that variable to `true`. This allows us to get rid of a few lines of code. Have a look at Listing 187, before you continue.

```
1  public boolean hasBad(String str) {
2    boolean result = false;
3    if (str.length() >= 3) {
4      result = result || helper(str, 0);
5    }
6    if (str.length() >= 4) {
7      result = result || helper(str, 1);
8    }
9    return result;
10 }
11
12 public boolean helper(String str, int pos) {
13   return (str.substring(pos, pos + 3).equals("bad"));
14 }
```

Listing 187: hasBad – variation 2

You have encountered the shorthand for adding to a variable already. For instance, instead of x = x + 1, you can also write x += 1. This works with boolean operators as well. The corresponding shorthand for the or-operator is |=. We can use

160

this to improve the solution. The outcome is that the one line that makes up the body of the two if-statement becomes a lot shorter. It gets even shorter if we abbreviate the name of the accumulator variable to `res`. Now look at the code in Listing 188. It is a quite significant improvement over the initial solution we have seen above in Listing 185. If you disagree, then think about what we would have to do in order to add extra cases. The code in Listing 188 would require just one extra line per case!

```java
public boolean hasBad(String str) {
  boolean res = false;
  if (str.length() >= 3) res |= helper(str, 0);
  if (str.length() >= 4) res |= helper(str, 1);
  return res;
}

public boolean helper(String str, int pos) {
  return (str.substring(pos, pos + 3).equals("bad"));
}
```

Listing 188: hasBad − variation 3

atFirst

Problem

The function `atFirst` takes a string `str` as its input. If `str` is at least two letters long, return a string consisting of the first two characters of that string. Otherwise, return a string of length 2 by appending the character `"@"` as necessary. The code skeleton is provided in Listing 189.

```
1 public String atFirst(String str) {
2 // your code here
3 }
```

Listing 189: atFirst – skeleton

Tools

For this problem, you will have to use conditional statements, the equals-operator (`==`), the string concatenation operator as well as the string methods `length` and `substring`.

Hints

This is a simple problem. Do not get led astray by trying to find a fancy solution. Instead, think about what you should do if the input string consists of the empty string. Treat that as one case. Then you will need another case if the input string consists of one character.

Solution

We start with the empty string. In that case, we return "@@". If the input string is of length 1, we append "@". Otherwise, we return a substring consisting of the first two characters of the input string `str`. The code is provided in Listing 190.

```
1 public String atFirst(String str) {
2   if (str.length() == 0) return "@@";
3   if (str.length() == 1) return str + "@";
4   return str.substring(0, 2);
5 }
```

Listing 190: atFirst – solution

You could of course try to dynamically determine how many "@" characters you need to append. This would be overkill in the given example, but if you were asked to return strings that are very long, that approach would clearly be preferable over manually specifying how to handle every single possible case.

lastChars

Problem

The function `lastChars` takes two strings a and b as input. It returns a string consisting of the first character of a and the last character of b. In case any of the input strings is empty, use the `'@'`-symbol in the output instead of that string. The code skeleton is given in Listing 191.

```
1 public String lastChars(String a, String b) {
2 // your code here
3 }
```

Listing 191: lastChars – skeleton

Tools

This problem requires the use of the string methods `length`, or `equals`, and `charAt`. Instead of the latter, you could also use `substring`. Furthermore, you will need to use conditional statements, boolean operators, the string concatenation operator, and comparison operators.

Hints

Start with a simple solution that covers all four possible cases, one after the other. Those cases are: a is empty and b is not, a is not empty and b is, both strings are empty, and, finally, none of the strings is empty.

Solution

A straightforward solution tackles all four cases in sequence, as shown in Listing 192. The code does not warrant much discussion as we simply check if the inputs are empty and if so, we use the '@' character in the output, according to the problem description. It may look strange that the empty string is used in two of the return statements. This is a convenient shorthand that converts a character into a string.

```java
public String lastChars(String a, String b) {
  if (a.length() == 0 && b.length() != 0) {
    return "@" + "" + b.charAt(b.length() - 1);
  }
  if (a.length() != 0 && b.length() == 0) {
    return a.charAt(0) + "@";
  }
  if (a.length() == 0 && b.length() == 0) {
    return "@@";
  }
  return a.charAt(0) + "" + b.charAt(b.length() - 1);
}
```

Listing 192: lastChars – solution

Discussion

You can probably already see that there are much more elegant ways to solve this problem. After all, there is significant redundancy in the code. Instead of checking four cases, we only need to check each string one single time and construct the string we want to return accordingly. This can be done conveniently with an accumulator variable. For added conciseness, the solution presented in Listing 193 uses the ternary operator and the string method `equals`.

```java
public String lastChars(String a, String b) {
  String res = "";
  res += a.equals("") ? "@" : a.charAt(0);
  res += b.equals("") ? "@" : b.charAt(b.length() - 1);
  return res;
}
```

Listing 193: lastChars – variation

conCat

Problem

The function conCat takes two strings a and b as its input. It returns the concatenation of a and b. However, if the first character of b is identical to the last character of a, one of those two characters is omitted. Either of the input strings could be empty. See Listing 194 for the code skeleton.

```
1 public String conCat(String a, String b) {
2 // your code here
3 }
```

Listing 194: conCat – skeleton

Tools

This problem requires the use of conditional statements, comparison operators, boolean operators, the string concatenation operators as well as the following string methods: equals, length, substring, and, optionally, charAt.

Hints

Break the problem down into cases and tackle them one by one, if you need to.

Solution

In order to avoid out-of-bounds errors, we first tackle cases where either of the input strings is empty. In that case, we return the concatenation of the input strings. If the function has not returned after that check, we know that neither of the input strings is empty. Thus, we can safely use the charAt method and return a new string that results from the concatenation of a and b, or a and a substring of b, starting from the first character. The code is shown in Listing 195.

```
1 public String conCat(String a, String b) {
2   if (a.equals("") || b.equals("")) {
3     return a + b;
4   }
5   // none of the strings is empty:
6   if (a.charAt(a.length() - 1) == b.charAt(0)) {
7     return a + b.substring(1);
8   }
9   return a + b;
10 }
```

Listing 195: conCat – solution

Discussion

Looking at the solution presented in Listing 194, you may notice that we return a + b in two cases. This hints at the existence of a possibility to condense the solution. As the code was presented, we cannot change the position of the first if-statement as we otherwise risk ending up with an out-of-bounds error. However, we can start with the case in which neither string is empty. This can be achieved by negating the first if-statement. The expression !(a.equals("") || b.equals("")) is rather unwieldy. However, an equivalent expression is !a.equals("") && !b.equals(""), which we use to arrive at a more elegant solution, is shown in Listing 196.

```
1 public String conCat(String a, String b) {
2   if (!a.equals("") && !b.equals("")) {
3     if (a.charAt(a.length() - 1) == b.charAt(0)) {
4       return a + b.substring(1);
5     }
6   }
7   return a + b;
8 }
```

Listing 196: conCat – variation

lastTwo

Problem

The function lastTwo takes a string str as its input and returns a new string that is identical to str, with the exception that the last two characters are swapped. If str is less than two characters long, return the empty string. The code skeleton is given in Listing 197.

```
1 public String lastTwo(String str) {
2 // your code here
3 }
```

Listing 197: lastTwo – skeleton

Tools

For this problem you will have to use a conditional statement, comparison operators as well as the following string methods: length, substring, and charAt .

Hints

This is a very straightforward problem. Start with the case of the input string being less than two characters long. With this case out of the way, you can safely use the string method charAt to index into the string.

Solution

This is a very simple problem. First, we check whether the input string str is less than two characters long. If so, we return str unchanged. Otherwise, we construct a new string, consisting of a substring of str that includes all but the last two characters as well as the last two characters with their respective position exchanged. The code is shown in Listing 198. For convenience, we use a separate variable l for storing the length of the input string str.

```
1  public String lastTwo(String str) {
2    int l = str.length();
3    if (l < 2) {
4      return str;
5    }
6    return str.substring(0, l - 2)
7            + str.charAt(l - 1)
8            + str.charAt(l - 2);
9  }
```

Listing 198: lastTwo – solution

seeColor

Problem

The function seeColor takes a string str as its input. If the first three letters of that string are equal to the string "red", return the string "red". If the first four letters of the string str are equal to the string "blue", return the string "blue". Otherwise, return the empty string. The input string can be of any length. You will find the code skeleton in Listing 199.

```
1 public String seeColor(String str) {
2 // your code here
3 }
```

Listing 199: seeColor – skeleton

Tools

You can use conditional statements, comparison operators, boolean operators as well as the following string methods: length, substring, and equals.

Hints

You have to take into account that the input string may be less than three or four characters long.

Solution

We have to tackle three cases. We first check whether the input string is at least of length 3 and that the first three characters are equal to the string "red". Then we repeat this, but with changed parameters: the string has to be of at least length 4, and the first four characters are compared with the string "blue". If none of those conditions are fulfilled, we return the empty string. The code is given in Listing 200.

```
1  public String seeColor(String str) {
2    if (str.length() >= 3 && str.substring(0, 3).equals("red"))
3      return "red";
4    if (str.length() >= 4 && str.substring(0, 4).equals("blue"))
5      return "blue";
6    return "";
7  }
```

Listing 200: seeColor – solution

Discussion

The code provided in Listing 200 is perfectly adequate. However, you may notice that there is significant repetition in it. This means that we can clean up the solution with a separate helper function that performs the required checks. This approach is shown in Listing 201. Note that we programmatically determine the required length, which is a safer approach as it is not error-prone, as opposed to supplying the length of the string s directly by hard-coding it.

```
1  public String seeColor(String str) {
2    if (helper(str, "red" )) return "red";
3    if (helper(str, "blue")) return "blue";
4    return "";
5  }
6
7  public boolean helper(String s, String c) {
8    int l = c.length();
9    return s.length() >= l && s.substring(0, l).equals(c);
10 }
```

Listing 201: seeColor – variation

frontAgain

Problem

The function `frontAgain` takes a string `str` as its input. Return `true` if the first two characters are equal to the last two characters, and `false` otherwise. Keep in mind that the input string may be less than two characters long. The code skeleton is given in Listing 202.

```
1 public boolean frontAgain(String str) {
2 // your code here
3 }
```

Listing 202: *frontAgain – skeleton*

Tools

You can use conditional statements, comparison operators, as well as the following string methods: `length`, `substring`, and `equals`.

Hints

Think about the corner case of the input string having insufficient length first.

Solution

In order to avoid out-of-bounds errors, we have to first tackle the case of the input string str having a length of less than 2. Afterwards, we construct a substring containing the first two as well as the last two characters. The code is provided in Listing 203. For improved readability, the substrings are stored in separate variables.

```java
public boolean frontAgain(String str) {
  int l = str.length();
  if (str.length() < 2) {
    return false;
  }
  String first = str.substring(0, 2);
  String last  = str.substring(l - 2);
  return first.equals(last);
}
```

Listing 203: frontAgain – solution

minCat

Problem

The function `minCat` takes two strings a and b as its input and returns their concatenation. However, if they are not of equal length, drop characters from the front of the longer string until they are of equal length. The code skeleton is given in Listing 204.

```
1 public String minCat(String a, String b) {
2 // your code here
3 }
```

Listing 204: minCat – skeleton

Tools

You will have to use conditional statements, comparison operators, arithmetic operators, the string concatenation operator and the following string methods: `length`, `substring`.

Hints

This is a slightly tricky problem. Try to figure out a way to determine the starting position of the substring of the longer string.

Solution

We can use the difference in length of the input string to determine the offset of the substring of the longer of the two input strings. Thus, if string a is longer than string b, the substring taken from b starts at whatever the value of the difference in length of the two strings is. In the case where b is longer than a, the same reasoning applies, just with a negated offset value. Lastly, there is no need to treat the case of both strings being of equal length as a third case. The offset is 0 in that case, which is covered by the catch-all case in the code shown in Listing 205.

```
1  public String minCat(String a, String b) {
2    int lenA = a.length();
3    int lenB = b.length();
4    int offset = lenA - lenB;
5    if (lenA > lenB) {
6      return a.substring(offset) + b;
7    }
8    return a + b.substring(-offset);
9  }
```

Listing 205: minCat – solution

extraFront

Problem

The function `extraFront` takes a string `str` as its input. Its output consists of a concatenation of three times the first two characters of the input string `str`. If the input string is less than two characters long, use the entire string for that operation. The code skeleton is provided in Listing 206.

```
1 public String extraFront(String str) {
2 // your code here
3 }
```

Listing 206: extraFront – skeleton

Tools

This problem requires the use of a conditional statement, comparison operators, the string concatenation operator as well as the string methods `length` and `substring`.

Hints

This is a very straightforward problem. Start with the case in which the input string `str` is less than two characters long.

Solution

One very clear approach consists of using a variable `front`, which contains the string we concatenate three copies of. If the input string `str` is less than two characters long, we assign `str` to the variable `front`. Otherwise, we assign a substring consisting of the first two characters of `str` to it. The resulting code is provided in Listing 207.

```
1  public String extraFront(String str) {
2    String front = "";
3    if (str.length() < 2) {
4      front = str;
5    } else {
6      front = str.substring(0, 2);
7    }
8    return front + front + front;
9  }
```

Listing 207: extraFront – solution

Discussion

This is the kind of problem that can be greatly condensed by using a ternary operator for determining which value to assign to a variable. For further conciseness, we could also use shorter variable name for the input string. The result of these modifications, shown in Listing 208, is a two-liner that is equivalent to the rather verbose solution we have seen above.

```
1  public String extraFront(String s) {
2    String front = (s.length() < 2) ? s : s.substring(0, 2);
3    return front + front + front;
4  }
```

Listing 208: extraFront – variation

without2

Problem

The function without2 takes a string str as its input. If the
last two characters of that string are identical to its first two
characters, return a substring of str that omits the first two
characters. The input string can be of any length. See Listing 209 for the code skeleton.

```
1 public String without2(String str) {
2 // your code here
3 }
```

Listing 209: without2 – skeleton

Tools

This problem requires the use of conditional statements in addition to comparison operators, arithmetic operators, and the
following string methods: length, equals, substring.

Hints

Start by breaking this problem down into the various cases you
have to solve.

Solution

Let us look at the possible cases of the input string. If the input string str is less than two characters long, we return the input string. Otherwise, we check if the first two characters of the input string are identical to its last two characters, and drop the first two characters. Lastly, all other cases lead us to returning the input string unchanged. See Listing 210 for the code. Note that the white space before calling the string method equals is ignored by the Java compiler.

```java
public String without2(String str) {
  int len = str.length();
  if (len < 2 ) {
    return str;
  } else if (str.substring(len - 2)
                 .equals(str.substring(0, 2))) {
    return str.substring(2);
  } else {
    return str;
  }
}
```

Listing 210: without2 – solution

Discussion

When looking at the solution above, you may have noticed that we return the same result in two different clauses. Consequently, the code would be a lot more elegant if we managed to get rid of one of them. However, due to how string indexing in Java is implemented, we would risk ending up with an out-of-bounds error if we did not tackle the corner case where the string is less than two characters long at first. There is another way to reroute the execution, namely by nesting the if-statements so that we first check that the input string is at least of length 2, and, if so, whether the first two characters of the input string match its last two characters. The code is provided in Listing 211.

181

```
1 public String without2(String str) {
2   int len = str.length();
3   if (len >= 2 ) {
4     if (str.substring(len - 2).equals(str.substring(0, 2))) {
5       return str.substring(2);
6     }
7   }
8   return str;
9 }
```

Listing 211: without2 – variation

deFront

Problem

The function deFront takes a string str as its input. It returns a new string that consists of all but the first two characters of that string. However, if the first character is equal to 'a', keep it. Also, keep the second character if it is equal to 'b'. The input string is at least two characters long. The code skeleton is provided in Listing 212.

```
1 public String deFront(String str) {
2 // your code here
3 }
```

Listing 212: deFront – skeleton

Tools

You will need conditional statements and the string concatenation operator. Furthermore, you will need to use the string methods charAt and substring.

Hints

Use an accumulator variable for the prefix, which you will prepend to the output. The prefix can have the values "", "a", "b", and "ab".

Solution

This is a fairly simple problem. Start by declaring an accumulator variable prefix, to which we add the characters 'a' and 'b', if they appear in the first and second position of the input string str, respectively. Afterwards, we return the concatenation of prefix and a substring of str that starts with the third character, if you count like a human, or the second one, if you count from 0. The code is presented in Listing 213.

```java
public String deFront(String str) {
  String prefix = "";
  if (str.charAt(0) == 'a') prefix += 'a';
  if (str.charAt(1) == 'b') prefix += 'b';
  return prefix + str.substring(2);
}
```

Listing 213: *deFront – solution*

startWord

Problem

The function startWord takes two strings str and word as its input. If the string word matches the start of str, return the former. If the first character of both strings is not identical, return word, but with the first character of str in place of the first character of word. The code skeleton is provided in Listing 214.

```
1 public String startWord(String str, String word) {
2 // your code here
3 }
```

Listing 214: startWord – skeleton

Tools

You will have to use conditional statements, comparison operators, and the following string methods: length, substring, equals, and charAt.

Hints

Extract substrings of the correct length, starting at the correct position, from str and compare them with the corresponding substring of word.

Solution

First, we have to exclude all cases where word is longer than str. Afterwards, we perform two comparisons. First we compare the beginning of str with word. Then we compare the beginning of str, minus the first character, with word, minus the first character. The code is given in Listing 215.

```java
public String startWord(String str, String word) {
  int word_len = word.length();
  if (word_len <= str.length()) {
    if (str.substring(0, word_len).equals(word))
      return word;
    if (str.substring(1, word_len).equals(word.substring(1)))
      return str.charAt(0) + word.substring(1);
  }
  return "";
}
```

Listing 215: deFront – solution

Discussion

Did you notice that some part of the code presented in Listing 215 is redundant? If not, then think about this: does the first character of word matter? The answer to that question is that it does not. If word is identical to the beginning of str, we return word, but if the first character of both strings differs, we use the first character of str in the return value. However, we use a character that is identical to the first value of str if word matches the beginning of str, because they are identical. Thus, we can drop the first of the two nested if statements altogether. The corresponding code is given in Listing 216.

```java
public String startWord(String str, String word) {
  int l = word.length();
  if (l <= str.length()
      && str.substring(1, l).equals(word.substring(1))) {
    return str.charAt(0) + word.substring(1);
  }
  return "";
}
```

Listing 216: deFront – variation

withoutX

Problem

The function `withoutX` takes a string `str` as its input. If the first or last character of `str` is equal to `'x'`, drop it. The code skeleton is given in Listing 217.

```
1  public String withoutX(String str) {
2  // your code here
3  }
```

Listing 217: withoutX – skeleton

Tools

For this problem, you can use conditional statements, comparison operators, the string concatenation operator as well as the following string methods: `length`, `charAt`, `substring`.

Hints

This is a tricky problem. Use either an accumulator variable or modify the variable `str` in place.

Solution

My approach is to modify the input string `str`. First, if `str` is the empty string, we return it right away. Otherwise, we check if the first character of `str` is equal to 'x'. If so, we reassign the substring of `str`, starting from position 1, to `str`. This potentially modifies the length of `str`. Consequently, the next check is for `str` being at least of length 1. If that is the case, we may perform another reassignment if the last character is equal to the character 'x'. The corresponding code is shown in Listing 218.

```
1  public String withoutX(String str) {
2    if (str.length() >= 1 ) {
3      if (str.charAt(0) == 'x') {
4        str = str.substring(1);
5      }
6      if (str.length() >= 1
7          && str.charAt(str.length() - 1) == 'x')  {
8        str = str.substring(0, str.length() - 1);
9      }
10   }
11   return str;
12 }
```

Listing 218: withoutX – solution

withoutX2

Problem

The function `withoutX2` takes a string `str` of arbitrary length as its input. If either of the first two characters of it is equal to `'x'`, return that string without those characters. Otherwise, return the string unchanged. The code skeleton is given in Listing 219.

```
1 public String withoutX2(String str) {
2 // your code here
3 }
```

Listing 219: *withoutX2 – skeleton*

Tools

For this problem you can use conditional statements, comparison operators, the string concatenation operator as well as the following string methods: `length`, `charAt`, and `substring`.

Hints

This problem is almost identical to the problem `deFront`.

Solution

This is a very straightforward problem. We start by declaring an accumulator variable `str`. If the input string `str` is at least of length 2, we check the first two characters in sequence. If any of those does not equal `'x'`, we append it to `res`. Afterwards, we append a substring of `str` starting at position 2 to `res`. The corresponding code is provided in Listing 220.

```java
public String withoutX2(String str) {
  String res = "";
  if (str.length() >= 2) {
    if (str.charAt(0) != 'x') res += str.charAt(0);
    if (str.charAt(1) != 'x') res += str.charAt(1);
    res += str.substring(2);
  }
  return res;
}
```

Listing 220: withoutX2 – solution

Array-1

firstLast6

Problem

The function `firstLast6` takes an array of integers `nums` as its input, which has a length of at least 1. Return `true` is the first and last element of this array are both equal to 6, and `false` otherwise. The code skeleton is provided in Listing 221.

```
1 public boolean firstLast6(int[] nums) {
2 // your code here
3 }
```

Listing 221: firstLast6 – skeleton

Tools

This problem requires array indexing, the array attribute `length`, comparison operators and boolean operators.

Hints

Look up how the necessary array operations work, if you are struggling.

Solution

We extract the first element in the array `nums` and assign it to the variable `first`. Afterwards, we do the same with the last element of the input array, assigning it to the variable `last`. As the final step, we determine if any of those two values is equal to 6. The code is provided in Listing 222. Of course, the code could be shortened to a one-liner.

```
1 public boolean firstLast6(int[] nums) {
2    int first = nums[0];
3    int last  = nums[nums.length - 1];
4    return first == 6 || last == 6;
5 }
```

Listing 222: firstLast6 – solution

sameFirstLast

Problem

The function `sameFirstLast` takes an array of integers `nums` as its input. Return `true` if the first and last element of the input array are identical, and `false` otherwise. Also return `false` if the input array is of length 0. The code skeleton is provided in Listing 223.

```
1 public boolean sameFirstLast(int[] nums) {
2 // your code here
3 }
```

Listing 223: sameFirstLast – skeleton

Tools

This problem requires a conditional statement, array indexing, the array attribute `length`, comparison operators, and boolean operators.

Hints

This problem is very similar to the previous one.

Solution

We first determine the length of the input string `nums`. If it is at least of length 1, we compare its first and last element. A final return statement takes care of the case where `nums` is of length 0. The corresponding code is given in Listing 224.

```
1 public boolean sameFirstLast(int[] nums) {
2    if (nums.length >= 1) {
3       return nums[0] == nums[nums.length - 1];
4    }
5    return false;
6 }
```

Listing 224: sameFirstLast – solution

makePi

Problem

The function `makePi` does not take any argument and returns an array containing, in order, the integers 3, 1, and 4. The code skeleton is provided in Listing 225.

```
1 public int[] makePi() {
2 // your code here
3 }
```

Listing 225: makePi skeleton

Tools

This problem only requires knowledge of array declaration and initialization.

Hints

You have to familiarize yourself with how to declare a pre-filled array. Alternatively, declare an empty array of length three and fill it with the desired values afterwards. Yes, this problem is really as simple as it sounds.

Solution

There are two ways of solving this problem. You either declare and initialize the array right away, or you declare an empty array of length 3 and fill it as needed. The first approach is shown in the code provided in Listing 226, while the second one is shown in the code in Listing 227.

```java
public int[] makePi() {
  int[] pie = { 3, 1, 4 };
  return pie;
}
```

Listing 226: makePi – solution

```java
public int[] makePi() {
  int[] pie = new int[3];
  pie[0] = 3;
  pie[1] = 1;
  pie[2] = 4;
  return pie;
}
```

Listing 227: makePi – variation

commonEnd

Problem

The function commonEnd takes two arrays of integers a and b as its input, which will at least be of length 1. Return true if they start with the same element or end with the same element, and false otherwise. The code skeleton is provided in Listing 228.

```
1 public boolean commonEnd(int[] a, int[] b) {
2 // your code here
3 }
```

Listing 228: commonEnd – skeleton

Tools

This problem requires array indexing, the array attribute length, comparison operators and boolean operators.

Hints

Start by thinking about which elements you need to compare and structure your code accordingly.

Solution

In order to arrive at a clean solution, we define a boolean variable sameFirst, which stores the result of comparing the first element of both arrays. Afterwards, we define a boolean variable sameLast, which does the same for the last element of both arrays. We finish by evaluating whether any of those two variables is true. The code is provided in Listing 229. Of course, you could turn this solution into a one-liner.

```java
public boolean commonEnd(int[] a, int[] b) {
    boolean sameFirst = a[0] == b[0];
    boolean sameLast  = a[a.length - 1] == b[b.length - 1];
    return  sameFirst || sameLast;
}
```

Listing 229: commonEnd – solution

sum3

Problem

The function sum3 takes an array of integers nums as its input, which contains exactly three elements. The goal is to return the sum of its elements. The code skeleton is provided in Listing 230.

```
1 public int sum3(int[] nums) {
2 // your code here
3 }
```

Listing 230: sum3 – skeleton

Tools

This problem requires array indexing and arithmetic operators. You are not supposed to use a for-loop.

Hints

At this point in this book, you should not have any problems with this exercise.

Solution

This is one of the most trivial problems in this book. It should have been much placed earlier in the introductory sequence on array problems. Anyway, we solve it quickly by indexing into the array at positions 1, 2, and 3 and summing up those elements. The code is provided in Listing 231.

```
1 public int sum3(int[] nums) {
2   return nums[0] + nums[1] + nums[2];
3 }
```

Listing 231: sum3 – solution

rotateLeft3

Problem

The function `rotateLeft3` takes an array of integers `nums` as its input, which contains exactly three elements. The goal is to left-rotate those elements by one, so that the first element appears in the last position, and the other elements each move one position to the left. The code skeleton is provided in Listing 232.

```
1 public int[] rotateLeft3(int[] nums) {
2 // your code here
3 }
```

Listing 232: rotateLeft3 – skeleton

Tools

This problem requires array indexing and array initialization.

Hints

Construct the array manually, similar to what you have done in `makePi`.

Solution

This is another very straightforward problem. We first declare and initialize and array, and fill it with the elements that appear, in this order, at positions 1, 2, and 0 in the input array nums. As a second step, we return the newly constructed array. See Listing 233 for the code.

```
1 public int[] rotateLeft3(int[] nums) {
2   int[] result = { nums[1], nums[2], nums[0] };
3   return result;
4 }
```

Listing 233: rotateLeft3 – solution

reverse3

Problem

The function `reverse3` takes an array of integers `nums` as its input, which contains exactly three elements. The goal is to reverse this array. The code skeleton is provided in Listing 234.

```
1 public int[] reverse3(int[] nums) {
2 // your code here
3 }
```

Listing 234: reverse3 – skeleton

Tools

This problem requires array indexing and array initialization.

Hints

Construct the array manually, similar to what we you have done in `makePi`.

Solution

I hope you do not find these problems too tedious. Just as in some of the previous ones, we constructs a new array by manually arranging its elements in the desired order. The code is shown in Listing 235.

```
1 public int[] reverse3(int[] nums) {
2    int[] result = { nums[2], nums[1], nums[0] };
3    return result;
4 }
```

Listing 235: reverse3 – solution

maxEnd3

Problem

The function maxEnd3 takes an array of integers nums as its input, which contains exactly three elements. Compare the first element of this array with its last element, and fill the entire array with whatever element is larger. The code skeleton is provided in Listing 236.

```
1 public int[] maxEnd3(int[] nums) {
2 // your code here
3 }
```

Listing 236: *maxEnd3 – skeleton*

Tools

This problem requires a conditional statement, comparison operators, and array assignment. Try to solve this problem first without using the inbuilt method Math.max.

Hints

Determine the largest element first. Then think about which elements you have to change.

Solution

We start with a more low-level solution that does not make use of the method Math.max. If the last element in this array is larger than the first one, we modify the first and second one. Otherwise, we modify the second and third one. The corresponding code is shown in Listing 237.

```
1  public int[] maxEnd3(int[] nums) {
2    if (nums[2] > nums[0]) {
3      nums[0] = nums[2];
4      nums[1] = nums[2];
5    } else{
6      nums[1] = nums[0];
7      nums[2] = nums[0];
8    }
9    return nums;
10 }
```

Listing 237: maxEnd3 – solution

Discussion

Of course, we can clean up the code. We could use the ternary operator to take care of determining the maximum value in one line. Afterwards, we return a new array instead of modifying the provided array in place. This leads to a much more concise version, which is shown in Listing 238.

```
1  public int[] maxEnd3(int[] nums) {
2    int    val    = (nums[0] > nums[2]) ? nums[0] : nums[2];
3    int[] result = { val, val, val };
4    return result;
5  }
```

Listing 238: maxEnd3 – variation

sum2

Problem

The function sum2 takes an array of integers nums as its input, which is of arbitrary length. Return the sum of the first two elements of this array. If any of those elements are missing, consider it to be 0 for the resulting sum. The code skeleton is given in Listing 239.

```
1 public int sum2(int[] nums) {
2 // your code here
3 }
```

Listing 239: sum2 – skeleton

Tools

This problem requires conditional statements, the array attribute length, comparison operators, array indexing, and arithmetic operators.

Hints

Take it one-by-one. Start with the case of the input array being of length 0.

Solution

We structure this problem around the length of the input array nums. If the input array nums is of length 0, we return 0. If it is of length 1, we return the value of the first element of the array. Otherwise, we return the sum of the first two elements of nums. The corresponding code is provided in Listing 240.

```java
public int sum2(int[] nums) {
    if (nums.length == 0) return 0;
    if (nums.length == 1) return nums[0];
    return nums[0] + nums[1];
}
```

Listing 240: sum2 – solution

middleWay

Problem

The function `middleWay` takes two arrays of integers a and b as its input, which are both of length 3. The goal is to return a new array, consisting of the middle elements of a and b, in that order. The code skeleton is given in Listing 241.

```
1 public int[] middleWay(int[] a, int[] b) {
2 // your code here
3 }
```

Listing 241: middleWay – skeleton

Tools

For this problem, you only have to know how to access elements in an array and how to declare and initialize an array.

Hints

This problem is very similar to several previous ones.

Solution

This problem should be very easy. We declare a new array, consisting of the middle elements of both input arrays, as shown in Listing 242.

```
1 public int[] middleWay(int[] a, int[] b) {
2   int[] result = { a[1], b[1] };
3   return result;
4 }
```

Listing 242: middleWay – solution

makeEnds

Problem

The function `makeEnds` takes an array of integers `nums` as its input. It contains at least one element. Return an array that contains the first as well as the last element of `nums`, in that order. The code skeleton is given in Listing 243.

```
1 public int[] makeEnds(int[] nums) {
2 // your code here
3 }
```

Listing 243: makeEnds – skeleton

Tools

For this problem, you have to know how to access elements in an array and how to declare and initialize an array. You also have to use the array attribute `length`.

Hints

This problem is very similar to several previous ones.

Solution

This is very straightforward. We declare a new array of integers result, which consists of the first element of nums, as well as the last element of that array, which we access by indexing into it, using the length attribute. We have to subtract 1 from that value, because in Java, the first element of the array is located at position 0. The code is provided in Listing 244.

```java
public int[] makeEnds(int[] nums) {
    int[] result = { nums[0], nums[nums.length - 1] };
    return result;
}
```

Listing 244: makeEnds – solution

has23

Problem

The function has23 takes an array of integers nums as its input, which contains two elements. Return true if that array contains the value 2 or 3 at least once. The code skeleton is given in Listing 245.

```
1  public boolean has23(int[] nums) {
2  // your code here
3  }
```

Listing 245: has23 skeleton

Tools

For this problem you can use boolean variables, boolean operators, comparison operators, and array indexing. You should not use a loop.

Hints

Start by declaring a variable has2 that is set to true if one of the two elements of the input array nums is equal to 2, and false otherwise. From then on, the remaining steps should be easy to see.

Solution

We use two boolean variables has2 and has3, which record whether the array contains a 2 or a 3, respectively. Since the array contains only two elements, we simply index into the array and check whether the elements at position 0 and 1 are equal to 2 or 3. The corresponding code is provided in Listing 246. Of course, you could turn the code into a less readable one-liner.

```
1 public boolean has23(int[] nums) {
2   boolean has2 = nums[0] == 2 || nums[1] == 2;
3   boolean has3 = nums[0] == 3 || nums[1] == 3;
4   return has2 || has3;
5 }
```

Listing 246: has23 – solution

no23

Problem

The function no23 takes an array of integers nums as its input, which contains two elements. Return true if that array contains neither the value 2 nor the value 3. The code skeleton is given in Listing 247.

```
1 public boolean no23(int[] nums) {
2 // your code here
3 }
```

Listing 247: no23 – skeleton

Tools

For this problem you can use boolean variables, boolean operators, comparison operators, and array indexing. You should not use a loop.

Hints

This problem is the inverse of the previous one, has23. Use the solution to that problem as the starting point.

Solution

We start with the solution to problem has23 and find the negation of the expressions used therein. This means that we first check that neither element is equal to 2, followed by checking that neither element is equal to 3. Afterwards, we return the conjunction (&&) of that problem. See Listing 248 for the code.

```java
public boolean no23(int[] nums) {
    boolean hasNo2 = nums[0] != 2 && nums[1] != 2;
    boolean hasNo3 = nums[0] != 3 && nums[1] != 3;
    return hasNo2 && hasNo3;
}
```

Listing 248: no23 – solution

makeLast

Problem

The function makeLast takes an array of integers nums as its
input. Return a new array that is twice as long as nums. It
has to contain zeroes throughout, with the exception of the last
element, which should be identical to the last element of the
array nums. The code skeleton is given in Listing 249.

```
1 public int[] makeLast(int[] nums) {
2 // your code here
3 }
```

Listing 249: makeLast − skeleton

Tools

For this problem you need to know how to declare and initialize
an array. Furthermore, you will have to use array indexing, array
mutation of values, arithmetic operators, and the array attribute
length.

Hints

Arrays are initialized to containing zeros in Java, which means
that you only need to modify the last value of the array you are
going to create.

Solution

The array we return has to be twice as long as the input array nums, so we use twice the length of nums for the initialization of the array result. Afterwards, we look up the value that is stored in the last position of nums and put the same value in the last position of the array result. See Listing 250 for the code.

```
1  public int[] makeLast(int[] nums) {
2      int[] result = new int[2 * nums.length];
3      result[result.length-1] = nums[nums.length - 1];
4      return result;
5  }
```

Listing 250: makeLast – solution

221

double23

Problem

The function `double23` takes an array of integers `nums` as its input, which contains at most two elements. Return `true` if that array contains the value 2 twice or the value 3 twice, and `false` otherwise. The code skeleton is given in Listing 251.

```
1 public boolean double23(int[] nums) {
2 // your code here
3 }
```

Listing 251: double23 – skeleton

Tools

You can use conditional statements, comparison operators, boolean operators, and array indexing.

Hints

Can an array of length 0 or 1 contain two elements?

Solution

First, we take care of cases where the input array is not of length 2. We know that such arrays cannot contain two values, so we return `false` right away. Afterwards, we set up two conditional statements for checking both values of the input array, one checking for the value 2, the other checking for the value 3. We return `true` if those conditions are met, and `false` otherwise. As a final catch-all statement, we return `false`. The corresponding code is provided in Listing 252.

```
1  public boolean double23(int[] nums) {
2    if (nums.length < 2)                    return false;
3    if (nums[0] == 2 && nums[1] == 2) return true;
4    if (nums[0] == 3 && nums[1] == 3) return true;
5    return false;
6  }
```

Listing 252: *double23 – skeleton*

Discussion

For a shorter solution, you can condense the last two lines into one, as shown in the variation in Listing 253. I would argue that the previous solution is cleaner, though.

```
1  public boolean double23(int[] nums) {
2    if (nums.length < 2)                    return false;
3    if (nums[0] == 2 && nums[1] == 2) return true;
4    return nums[0] == 3 && nums[1] == 3;
5  }
```

Listing 253: *double23 – variation*

223

fix23

Problem

The function `fix23` takes an array of integers `nums` as its input, which contains three elements. Do the following for every element in the array: If the element is equal to 2, and the subsequent element is equal to 3, replace the latter with 0. Return the modified array. The code skeleton is given in Listing 254.

```
1 public int[] fix23(int[] nums) {
2 // your code here
3 }
```

Listing 254: fix23 – skeleton

Tools

You can use conditional statements, comparison operators, boolean operators, array indexing, and array assignment.

Hints

You need to consider only two cases. You can ignore out-of-bounds issues because we know that the array is of length 3.

Solution

The condition described in the problem statement implies that there are two cases we need to consider. First, we check whether the first element in the array is equal to 2 and followed by 3, afterwards we check whether the second element of the input array is equal to 2 and followed by a 3. If any of those conditions are met, we modify the latter element. The code is given in Listing 255.

```
1 public int[] fix23(int[] nums) {
2   if (nums[0] == 2 && nums[1] == 3) nums[1] = 0;
3   if (nums[1] == 2 && nums[2] == 3) nums[2] = 0;
4   return nums;
5 }
```

Listing 255: fix23 – solution

start1

Problem

The function start1 takes two arrays of integers a and b as its
input. Return how many of those arrays start with the element
1. The code skeleton is given in Listing 256.

```
1 public int start1(int[] a, int[] b) {
2 // your code here
3 }
```

Listing 256: start1 – skeleton

Tools

You can use conditional statements, comparison operators, boolean
operators, array indexing, and arithmetic operators.

Hints

Use an accumulator variable that records the number of arrays
that start with 1.

Solution

We declare an integer variable count, which we will use as an accumulator. It is initialized to 0 and increased by 1 if the input arrays a and b, respectively, start with 1. Of course, due to the problem of out-of-bounds errors the subsequent conditional statements have to be set up in a way that precludes arrays of length 0. The code is given in Listing 257. On a side note, instead of writing count += 1, you could also write count++.

```java
public int start1(int[] a, int[] b) {
    int count = 0;
    if (a.length > 0 && a[0] == 1) count += 1;
    if (b.length > 0 && b[0] == 1) count += 1;
    return count;
}
```

Listing 257: start1 – solution

biggerTwo

Problem

The function `biggerTwo` takes two arrays of integers a and b as its input, which are both of length 2. Sum up the elements of the arrays and return the array whose elements sum up to a larger value. If that value is the same for both arrays, return array a. The code skeleton is provided in Listing 258.

```
1 public int[] biggerTwo(int[] a, int[] b) {
2 // your code here
3 }
```

Listing 258: biggerTwo – skeleton

Tools

You can use conditional statements, comparison operators, array indexing, and arithmetic operators.

Hints

Index into the arrays and sum up the elements one by one.

Solution

This problem boils down to a single if-statement. We sum up all elements of array a as well as all elements of array b. After comparing the resulting value, we know which array we have to return. The code is provided in Listing 259.

```
1 public int[] biggerTwo(int[] a, int[] b) {
2   if (a[0] + a[1] < b[0] + b[1]) return b;
3   return a;
4 }
```

Listing 259: biggerTwo – solution

Discussion

This problem is also a good example for the benefits of the ternary operator. In this case, it leads to more elegant code, as you can see in Listing 260

```
1 public int[] biggerTwo(int[] a, int[] b) {
2   return (a[0] + a[1] < b[0] + b[1]) ? b : a;
3 }
```

Listing 260: biggerTwo – variation

makeMiddle

Problem

The function `makeMiddle` takes an arrays of integers `nums` as its input, which is of even length and contains at least two elements. Return an array that contains the middle two elements of `nums`. The code skeleton is provided in Listing 261.

```
1 public int[] makeMiddle(int[] nums) {
2 // your code here
3 }
```

Listing 261: makeMiddle – skeleton

Tools

For this problem, you will need to use the array attribute `length`, array indexing, arithmetic operators as well as array declaration and initialization.

Hints

Think about how you can use the array attribute `length` to determine which array elements you need.

Solution

In an array of even length, there are two middle elements. The second one of those elements of an array `nums` is at position `nums.length / 2`. The first one of the middle elements is located one to the left of that position, so we only need to subtract 1 from it. Thus, we can directly construct a new array of two elements that contains the two middle elements of the input array `nums`, as shown in Listing 262.

```
1 public int[] makeMiddle(int[] nums) {
2    int    mid    = nums.length / 2;
3    int[] result = {nums[mid - 1], nums[mid]};
4    return result;
5 }
```

Listing 262: makeMiddle – solution

plusTwo

Problem

The function `plusTwo` takes two arrays of integers `a` and `b` as its input, which are both of length 2. Return a new array that contains the elements of `a` and `b`, in this order. The code skeleton is provided in Listing 263.

```
1 public int[] plusTwo(int[] a, int[] b) {
2 // your code here
3 }
```

Listing 263: plusTwo – skeleton

Tools

For this problem, you will need to use array indexing as well as array declaration and initialization.

Hints

This problem is similar to previous ones, such as `middleWay`.

Solution

This is a very straightforward problem. We first declare an array and initialize it, in this order, with the values of the input arrays a and b. Afterwards, we return that array. The code is provided in Listing 264.

```java
public int[] plusTwo(int[] a, int[] b) {
    int[] result = { a[0], a[1], b[0], b[1] };
    return result;
}
```

Listing 264: plusTwo – solution

swapEnds

Problem

The function `swapEnds` takes an array of integers `nums` of length 2 as its input. Return that array, but with its first and last element swapped. The code skeleton is provided in Listing 265.

```
1 public int[] swapEnds(int[] nums) {
2 // your code here
3 }
```

Listing 265: *swapEnds – skeleton*

Tools

For this problem, you will need to use array indexing and the array attribute `length`.

Hints

You can modify the array `nums` in place, which means that you do not need to create a new array.

Solution

Let us start by declaring two integer variables `first` and `last`, to which we assign the first and last element of the input array `nums`, respectively. Afterwards, we change the elements in the first and last positions of the input array. The corresponding code is provided in Listing 266.

```
1  public int[] swapEnds(int[] nums) {
2    int first = nums[0];
3    int last  = nums[nums.length - 1];
4    nums[0]               = last;
5    nums[nums.length - 1] = first;
6    return nums;
7  }
```

Listing 266: swapEnds – solution

Discussion

Alternatively, you could shorten the code by one line as it is not necessary to store the values of both positions in separate variables. Instead, declare a temporary variable `tmp` for the first element of the input array `nums`. Afterwards, assign the value of the last element of `nums` to the first position of that array. As a last step, assign the value that is stored in `tmp` to the last position in the array `nums`. The code is shown in Listing 267.

```
1  public int[] swapEnds(int[] nums) {
2    int tmp = nums[0];
3    nums[0] = nums[nums.length - 1];
4    nums[nums.length - 1] = tmp;
5    return nums;
6  }
```

Listing 267: swapEnds – variation

midThree

Problem

The function `midThree` takes an arrays of integers `nums` as its input, which is of odd length and contains at least three elements. Return an array that contains the middle three elements of `nums`. The code skeleton is provided in Listing 268.

```
1 public int[] midThree(int[] nums) {
2 // your code here
3 }
```

Listing 268: midThree – skeleton

Tools

For this problem, you will need to use the array attribute `length`, array indexing, arithmetic operators as well as array declaration and initialization.

Hints

This problem is very similar to `makeMiddle`.

Solution

In an array of odd length of at least length 3, there are three middle elements. The element right in the middle is at position `length / 2`. Once we have determined that position, we only have to look one position to the left and one to the right of it to find the other two elements. Afterwards, we construct a new array, consisting of the three elements thus identified. See Listing 269 for the code.

```
1 public int[] midThree(int[] nums) {
2   int mid = nums.length / 2;
3   int[] result = { nums[mid - 1], nums[mid], nums[mid + 1] };
4   return result;
5 }
```

Listing 269: midThree – solution

maxTriple

Problem

The function `maxTriple` takes an arrays of integers `nums` as its input, which is of odd length and contains at least one element. Return an integer that represents the maximum value of the first, middle, and last element of `nums`. The code skeleton is provided in Listing 270.

```
1 public int maxTriple(int[] nums) {
2 // your code here
3 }
```

Listing 270: maxTriple – skeleton

Tools

You can use conditional statements, array indexing, comparison operators and the array attribute `length`. Do not use the method `Math.max`.

Hints

Compare the candidate elements one after the other.

Solution

We start by extracting the middle and last element of the array. Afterwards, we declare a variable max, which we initialize to the first element of the array. At this point, this is merely a guess. Afterwards, we compare max sequentially to the middle and last element and assign any of those elements to max if it is larger as the current value of that variable. See Listing 271 for the code.

```java
public int maxTriple(int[] nums) {
  int mid = nums.length / 2;
  int end = nums.length - 1;
  int max = nums[0];
  if (nums[mid] > max) max = nums[mid];
  if (nums[end] > max) max = nums[end];
  return max;
}
```

Listing 271: maxTriple – solution

239

frontPiece

Problem

The function `frontPiece` takes an arrays of integers `nums` as its input, which is of arbitrary length. Return an array containing the first two elements of that array. If the array contains less than two elements, return the entire array. The code skeleton is provided in Listing 272.

```
1  public int[] frontPiece(int[] nums) {
2  // your code here
3  }
```

Listing 272: frontPiece – skeleton

Tools

You can use conditional statements, array indexing, comparison operators and the array attribute `length`.

Hints

This problem is similar to several previous ones.

Solution

In order to avoid out-of-bounds errors, we first tackle the case of the input array nums containing less than two elements. If the function has not triggered that return statement, we know that the array contains at least two elements. Thus, we can construct a new array that consists of the first two elements of nums. The code is provided in Listing 273.

```java
public int[] frontPiece(int[] nums) {
    if (nums.length < 2) return nums;
    int[] result = { nums[0], nums[1] };
    return result;
}
```

Listing 273: frontPiece – solution

unlucky1

Problem

The function `unlucky1` takes an array of integers `nums` as its input, which is of arbitrary length. For this problem, a 1 is *unlucky* if it is followed immediately by a 3. Return `true` if the array `nums` contains an unlucky 1 in the first two or last two positions, and `false` otherwise. The code skeleton is provided in Listing 274.

```
1 public boolean unlucky1(int[] nums) {
2 // your code here
3 }
```

Listing 274: *unlucky1 – skeleton*

Tools

You can use conditional statements, array indexing, comparison operators and the array attribute `length`.

Hints

In how many and which positions of the array could an unlucky 1 show up?

Solution

An important insight is that there are only three positions in which an unlucky 1 could show up, namely the first, second, and second-to-last position in the input array nums. Thus, after taking care of the case where the input array contains less than two elements, we turn our attention to the potential positions of unlucky ones. Each requires a simple if-statement that checks if a 1 is followed by a 3. See Listing 275 for the code.

```java
public boolean unlucky1(int[] nums) {
  int l = nums.length;
  if (l < 2)                                return false;
  if (nums[0]   == 1 && nums[1]   == 3) return true;
  if (nums[1]   == 1 && nums[2]   == 3) return true;
  if (nums[l-2] == 1 && nums[l-1] == 3) return true;
  return false;
}
```

Listing 275: unlucky1 – solution

243

make2

Problem

The function `make2` takes two arrays of integers a and b as its input. Together, those two arrays contain at least 2 elements. The goal is to return an array of length 2 that contains as many elements of a as possible. If there are not enough elements in a, use elements from b. The code skeleton is provided in Listing 276.

```
1 public int[] make2(int[] a, int[] b) {
2 // your code here
3 }
```

Listing 276: make2 – skeleton

Tools

You can use conditional statements, array indexing, comparison operators and the array attribute `length`.

Hints

Which elements do you have to return if the input array a is empty? Which if it contains only 1 element?

Solution

We first declare and initialize an array of length 2. Afterwards, we use separate if-statements to take care of these three cases: the input array a is of length 0, the input array a is of length 1, and, finally, all other cases. In the first case, we take the first two elements of array b. In the second case, we take the first element of a as well as the first element of b. In the final case, we take the first two elements of a. See Listing 277 for the code.

```
1  public int[] make2(int[] a, int[] b) {
2    int[] res = new int[2];
3    if (a.length == 0) {
4      res[0] = b[0];
5      res[1] = b[1];
6    } else if (a.length == 1) {
7      res[0] = a[0];
8      res[1] = b[0];
9    } else{
10     res[0] = a[0];
11     res[1] = a[1];
12   }
13   return res;
14 }
```

Listing 277: make2 – solution

Discussion

Looking at the if-statements, you may notice that there are only two possible candidates for the first element. Thus, it is possible to shorten the code a little bit. Have a look at Listing 278 for a variation of the solution. The nested ternary operator is more for my own entertainment. You should not do that in production code. Also, notice that the more verbose solution in Listing 277 is arguably a lot more readable.

```
1 public int[] make2(int[] a, int[] b) {
2   int l      = a.length;
3   int first  = l == 0 ? b[0] : a[0];
4   int second = l == 0 ? b[1] : (l == 1 ? b[0] : a[1]);
5   int[] res = { first, second };
6   return res;
7 }
```

Listing 278: make2 – variation

front11

Problem

The function front11 takes two arrays of integers a and b as its input, which are of arbitrary length. Return an array containing the first element of each array, in the given order. If any of those arrays does not contain any elements, ignore it. The code skeleton is provided in Listing 279.

```
1 public int[] front11(int[] a, int[] b) {
2 // your code here
3 }
```

Listing 279: front11 – skeleton

Tools

You can use conditional statements, array indexing, comparison operators and the array attribute length.

Hints

Approach this problem with a nested if-statement. First, distinguish between between the case where the input array a has length 0 and all other cases. Afterwards, consider the length of array b separately in each case.

Solution

This is a somewhat tedious problem. We have to consider a total of four cases: array a has length 0, while array b has either length 0 (case 1) or a length greater than 0 (case 2). Array a may also have a length greater than 0, while array b has a length of 0 (case 3) or a length greater than 0 (case 4). After setting up a nested if-statement that takes those four cases into account, the remaining code essentially writes itself as we only need to construct the array that has to be returned, according to the case we are in. See Listing 280 for the code.

```
 1  public int[] front11(int[] a, int[] b) {
 2    if (a.length == 0) {
 3      if (b.length == 0) {
 4        return a;
 5      } else {
 6        int[] res = { b[0] };
 7        return res;
 8      }
 9    } else { // a.length >= 1
10      if (b.length == 0) {
11        int[] res = { a[0] };
12        return res;
13      } else {
14        int[] res = { a[0], b[0] };
15        return res;
16      }
17    }
18  }
```

Listing 280: front11 – solution

Logic-1

cigarParty

Problem

The function `cigarParty` takes an integer `cigars` and a boolean `isWeekend` as its input. If the value of `isWeekend` is true, return true if the value of `cigars` is greater than 40, and `false` otherwise. If the value of `isWeekend` is `false`, return true if the value of `cigars` is in the range [40 ... 60], and `false` otherwise. The code skeleton is provided in Listing 281.

```
1 public boolean cigarParty(int cigars, boolean isWeekend) {
2 // your code here
3 }
```

Listing 281: *cigarParty – skeleton*

Tools

You can use conditional statements, comparison operators, and boolean operators.

Hints

Translate the problem statements one-by-one into if-statements.

Solution

We first check if the boolean isWeekend is true. If that is the case, we check that the value of the integer variable cigars is greater than 40, and we are done. If the variable isWeekend is false, we check that the value of cigars is between 40 and 60, inclusive. The corresponding code is given in Listing 282.

```
1 public boolean cigarParty(int cigars, boolean isWeekend) {
2   if (isWeekend) {
3     return (cigars >= 40);
4   }
5   return cigars >= 40 && cigars <= 60;
6 }
```

Listing 282: cigarParty – solution

Discussion

Notice that we check that the value of cigars is at least 40 in any case. The variable isWeekend merely determines if we also check an upper bound of the provided integer. Thus, the code can be simplified and turned into a one-liner. The conjunction in Listing 283 checks that cigars is at most 60 if isWeekend is false. Otherwise, that expression evaluates to true.

```
1 public boolean cigarParty(int cigars, boolean isWeekend) {
2   return cigars >= 40 && (!isWeekend ? cigars <= 60 : true);
3 }
```

Listing 283: cigarParty – variation

dateFashion

Problem

The function dateFashion takes two integers you and date as its input, which record how fashionable, on a scale from 0 to 10, both you and your date are. The output of this function determines whether you get into a fancy venue. Possible values are 0 (no), 1 (maybe), and 2 (yes). If both inputs are 2 or less, return 0. If one of the inputs is at least 8 and the other is greater than 2, return 2. In all other cases, return 1. The code skeleton is provided in Listing 284.

```
1 public int dateFashion(int you, int date) {
2 // your code here
3 }
```

Listing 284: dateFashion – skeleton

Tools

You can use conditional statements, comparison operators, and boolean operators.

Hints

Translate the problem statements into separate if-statements.

Solution

Use the wording in the problem description as a guide and set up three if-statements. First, we check if one of the input values you and date is less than 2. Then, we check if one of the two input values is at least 8 and the other greater than 2. In the provided solution, this is done in two separate if-statements, but they could of course be combined into one. Lastly, we return 1 as a final statement. See Listing 285 for the code.

```
1 public int dateFashion(int you, int date) {
2    if (you  <= 2 || date <= 2) return 0;
3    if (you  >= 8 && date >  2) return 2;
4    if (date >= 8 && you  >  2) return 2;
5    return 1;
6 }
```

Listing 285: dateFashion — solution

squirrelPlay

Problem

The function `squirrelPlay` takes an integer `temp` (temperature) and a boolean `isSummer` as its input. This function determines if squirrels play. They play if `temp` is at least 60 but at most, if `isSummer` is true, 100. Otherwise, the upper limit of the range is 90. The code skeleton is provided in Listing 286.

```
1 public boolean squirrelPlay(int temp, boolean isSummer) {
2 // your code here
3 }
```

Listing 286: squirrelPlay – skeleton

Tools

You can use conditional statements, comparison operators, and boolean operators.

Hints

Translate the problem statements into separate if-statements.

Solution

The lower limit of the range is fixed. Thus, we can return `false` if the value of `temp` is not at least 60. If that value is at least 60, on the other hand, we check the value of the boolean variable `isSummer` and set it to 100 or 90. See Listing 287 for the code.

```
1 public boolean squirrelPlay(int temp, boolean isSummer) {
2   if (temp >= 60) {
3     return isSummer ? temp <= 100 : temp <= 90;
4   }
5   return false;
6 }
```

Listing 287: squirrelPlay – solution

Discussion

If you have a keen eye, you may realize that there is some repetition in the code above. Indeed, we can condense the check of the upper limit by factoring out the left side of the comparison together with the comparison operator. Listing 288 shows how to do this.

```
1 public boolean squirrelPlay(int temp, boolean isSummer) {
2   return temp >= 60 && temp <= (isSummer ? 100 : 90);
3 }
```

Listing 288: squirrelPlay – variation

caughtSpeeding

Problem

The function `caughtSpeeding` takes an integer speed and a boolean `isBirthday` as its input. This function determines the fine for speeding as an integer, ranging from none (0) to minor (1) to major (2). If the value of speed is at most 60, there is no fine. If the value of speed is above 60 and at most 80, a minor fine will be due. Lastly, if speed is above 80, a major fine will be due. There is one caveat, though: If `isBirthday` is `true`, the bounds 60 and 80 will be changed to 65 and 85. The code skeleton is provided in Listing 289.

```
1 public int caughtSpeeding(int speed, boolean isBirthday) {
2 // your code here
3 }
```

Listing 289: `caughtSpeeding` – skeleton

Tools

You can use conditional statements, comparison operators, and arithmetic operators.

Hints

This is a potentially convoluted problem. Thus, I would suggest that you first check the value of the variable `isBirthday`. If that value is `true`, modify the value of the variable `speed`.

Solution

In order to arrive at a straightforward solution, we subtract 5 from the input value speed if isBirthday is true. Afterwards, we use two conditional statements to determine in which interval the potentially modified value of speed resides. See Listing 290 for the code.

```
1 public int caughtSpeeding(int speed, boolean isBirthday) {
2   if (isBirthday)  speed -= 5;
3   if (speed <= 60) return 0;
4   return (speed <= 80) ? 1 : 2;
5 }
```

Listing 290: caughtSpeeding – solution

sortaSum

Problem

The function sortaSum takes two integers a and b as its input. If their sum lies in the interval [10 ... 19], return 20. Otherwise, return their sum. The code skeleton is provided in Listing 291.

```
1 public int sortaSum(int a, int b) {
2 // your code here
3 }
```

Listing 291: sortaSum – skeleton

Tools

You can use conditional statements, comparison operators, boolean operators, and arithmetic operators.

Hints

This is a simple problem that boils down to just one conditional statement.

Solution

We first compute the sum of the input values a and b. Afterwards, we check if that sum is in the range specified above. If that is the case, we return 20. Otherwise, we return the sum we just computed. For conciseness, the code in Listing 292 makes use of the ternary operator.

```java
public int sortaSum(int a, int b) {
  int sum = a + b;
  return (sum >= 10 && sum <= 19) ? 20 : sum;
}
```

Listing 292: sortaSum – solution

alarmClock

Problem

The function `alarmClock` takes an integer day and a boolean `vacation` as its input. Its return value is a string that indicates when we should get up. The value of the variable day ranges from 0 to 6 and represents the day of the week, starting with Sunday, which is represented by 0. Indicate when the alarm clock should ring, based on the following rules. If `vacation` is `false` and it is a weekday, we have to get up at "7:00", but if it is the weekend, we want to get up at "10:00". On the other hand, if `vacation` is `true`, we get up on "10:00" on a weekday. On the weekend, we will not bother with an alarm clock. In that case, the value is "off". The code skeleton is provided in Listing 293.

```
1 public String alarmClock(int day, boolean vacation) {
2 // your code here
3 }
```

Listing 293: *alarmClock – skeleton*

Tools

You can use conditional statements, comparison operators, and boolean operators.

Hints

For this problem it would help a lot if you used ternary operators to encode the conditions. Afterwards, check first if the provided value for day is a weekday.

Solution

This problem could be solved with a rather unsightly nested if-statement. However, by using the ternary operator, we turn it into just three lines of code. Structurally, we first check if the provided value for day is in the range [1 ... 5]. Afterwards, we check, for each outcome, the value of the variable vacation, and return the appropriate value. A concise solution is given in Listing 294.

```
1  public String alarmClock(int day, boolean vacation) {
2    String weekday = vacation ? "10:00" : "7:00";
3    String weekend = vacation ? "off"   : "10:00";
4    return (day >= 1 && day <= 5) ? weekday : weekend;
5  }
```

Listing 294: alarmClock – solution

Discussion

If you have not yet gotten used to the ternary operator, you may appreciate the more verbose solution provided in Listing 295. The underlying program logic is exactly the same as in Listing 294.

```
1  public String alarmClock(int day, boolean vacation) {
2    if (day >= 1 && day <= 5) {
3      if (vacation) {
4        return "10:00";
5      } else {
6        return "7:00";
7      }
8    } else { // weekend
9      if (vacation) {
10       return "off";
11     }
12     return "10:00";
13   }
14 }
```

Listing 295: alarmClock – variation

love6

Problem

The function love6 takes two integers a and b as its input. Return true if any of the following conditions is fulfilled: Either a or b is equal to 6, the sum of a and b is equal to 6, or, lastly, the absolute difference of a and b is equal to 6. Otherwise, return false. The code skeleton is provided in Listing 296.

```
1 public boolean love6(int a, int b) {
2 // your code here
3 }
```

Listing 296: love6 – skeleton

Tools

You can use conditional statements, comparison operators, and boolean operators. You may also use the method Math.abs.

Hints

Set up a separate if-statement for each condition. You may use the method Math.abs, but you may want to instead think about how to solve this problem without it.

Solution

According to the problem statement, there are four conditions we have to check. We will do so one by one. If any of those conditions is met, we return `true`. Otherwise, as a catch-all statement, we return `false`. The code shown in Listing 297 does not use the method `Math.abs`.

```
1 public boolean love6(int a, int b) {
2   if (a == 6)      return true;
3   if (b == 6)      return true;
4   if (a + b == 6) return true;
5   if (a - b == 6) return true;
6   if (b - a == 6) return true;
7   return false;
8 }
```

Listing 297: love6 – solution

Discussion

For the sake of completeness, let us look at how to solve this problem with the method `Math.abs`. See Listing 298 for the code.

```
1 public boolean love6(int a, int b) {
2   if (a == 6)      return true;
3   if (b == 6)      return true;
4   if (a + b == 6) return true;
5   if (Math.abs(a - b) == 6) return true;
6   return false;
7 }
```

Listing 298: love6 – variation 1

Of course, you could condense the code even further as a one-liner, which is shown in Listing 299. The disadvantage of that approach is that the resulting code is not as easy to read.

```
1 public boolean love6(int a, int b) {
2   return a == 6 || b == 6 || a + b == 6
3          || Math.abs(a - b) == 6;
4 }
```

Listing 299: love6 – variation 2

in1To10

Problem

The function in1To10 takes an integer n as well as a boolean outsideMode as its input. If the value of outsideMode is true, return true if n is not in the range [1 ... 10], and false otherwise. If outsideMode is false, then return true if the value of n is within the range [1 ... 10], and false otherwise. The code skeleton is provided in Listing 300.

```
1 public boolean in1To10(int n, boolean outsideMode) {
2 // your code here
3 }
```

Listing 300: in1To10 – skeleton

Tools

You can use conditional statements, comparison operators, and boolean operators.

Hints

You only need to translate the textual description given above into code.

Solution

Based on the problem description given earlier, we set up an if-statement that checks whether the value of the boolean variable outsideMode is true. Depending on the outcome of that check, we determine if the value of the variable n is either within the range [1 ... 10] or outside of it. Refer to Listing 301 for the code.

```
1 public boolean in1To10(int n, boolean outsideMode) {
2   if (outsideMode) {
3     return n <= 1 || n >= 10;
4   } else {
5     return n >= 1 && n <= 10;
6   }
7 }
```

Listing 301: in1To10 – solution

specialEleven

Problem

The function `specialEleven` takes an integer n as its input. Return true if the value of n is either a multiple of 11 or one more than a multiple of 11. The code skeleton is provided in Listing 302.

```
1 public boolean specialEleven(int n) {
2 // your code here
3 }
```

Listing 302: specialEleven – skeleton

Tools

You can use conditional statements, comparison operators, and boolean operators. In addition, you will need to use the modulo operator (%).

Hints

For this problem you need to understand what the modulo operator expresses. If a number n is a multiple of a number m, then the result of the operation n % m is 0. You can probably see what the result would have to be if n is one more than a multiple of m.

Solution

The solution to this problem is a straightforward one-liner. We check if n % 11 is equal to 0 or equal to 1, and we are done. Refer to Listing 303 for the code.

```java
1 public boolean specialEleven(int n) {
2   return n % 11 == 0 || n % 11 == 1;
3 }
```

Listing 303: *specialEleven – solution*

more20

Problem

The function `more20` takes an integer `n` as its input. Return true if the value of `n` is one more or two more than a multiple of 20. The code skeleton is provided in Listing 304.

```
1 public boolean more20(int n) {
2 // your code here
3 }
```

Listing 304: more20 – skeleton

Tools

You can use conditional statements, comparison operators, and boolean operators. In addition, you will need to use the modulo operator (%).

Hints

This problem is very similar to the previous one, in1To10.

Solution

This is a simple problem. We only need to check if n % 20 is equal to 1 or equal to 2. Refer to Listing 305 for the code.

```java
public boolean more20(int n) {
  return n % 20 == 1 || n % 20 == 2;
}
```

Listing 305: more20 – solution

old35

Problem

The function old35 takes an integer n as its input. Return true if the value of n is either a multiple of 3 or a multiple of 5. The code skeleton is provided in Listing 306.

```
1 public boolean old35(int n) {
2 // your code here
3 }
```

Listing 306: old35 – skeleton

Tools

You can use conditional statements, comparison operators, and boolean operators. In addition, you will need to use the modulo operator (%).

Hints

Read the instruction carefully! If n is a multiple of both 3 and 5, the return value is false.

Solution

Let us start with a more verbose solution. First, we check that n is a multiple of 3 but not a multiple of 5. Afterwards, we do the opposite, i.e. we check whether n is a multiple of 5 but not of 3. At the very last, we return `false` as a catch-all statement. Refer to Listing 307 for the code.

```
1  public boolean old35(int n) {
2    if (n % 3 == 0 && n % 5 != 0) return true;
3    if (n % 3 != 0 && n % 5 == 0) return true;
4    return false;
5  }
```

Listing 307: old35 – solution

Discussion

As you can see, the check in the provided solution is for an either-or condition. Java has an obscure operator for that (^), which allows us to reduce the code to a one-liner, as shown in Listing 308.

```
1  public boolean old35(int n) {
2    return n % 3 == 0 ^ n % 5 == 0;
3  }
```

Listing 308: old35 – variation

273

less20

Problem

The function less20 takes an integer n as its input. Return true if the value of n is 1 or 2 less than a multiple of 20. The code skeleton is provided in Listing 309.

```
1 public boolean less20(int n) {
2 // your code here
3 }
```

Listing 309: less20 – skeleton

Tools

You can use conditional statements, comparison operators, and boolean operators. In addition, you will need to use the modulo operator (%).

Hints

What is the modulo of a number that is a multiple of 1 less than 20?

Solution

This is a potentially tricky problem if you have not yet gotten familiar with modulo arithmetic. First, you have to figure out that a number that is 1 less than a multiple of 2 will have a remainder of 19 after taking the modulo of 20. Similarly, a number that is 2 less than a multiple of 20 has a remainder of 18 after taking the modulo of 20. Now we know enough to solve this problem as we only have to translate those observations into code. See Listing 310 for the solution.

```
1 public boolean less20(int n) {
2   return n % 20 == 19 || n % 20 == 18;
3 }
```

Listing 310: less20 – solution

Discussion

There is an equivalent expression, which some of you may find more elegant. It is based on the observation that if we added 1 or 2 to n, we could check whether n % 20 is equal to 0. See Listing 311 for the corresponding code.

```
1 public boolean less20(int n) {
2   return (n + 1) % 20 == 0 || (n + 2) % 20 == 0;
3 }
```

Listing 311: less20 – variation

nearTen

Problem

The function `nearTen` takes an integer n as its input. Return true if the value of n is within 2 of a multiple of 10. The code skeleton is provided in Listing 312.

```
1 public boolean nearTen(int num) {
2 // your code here
3 }
```

Listing 312: nearTen – skeleton

Tools

You can use conditional statements, comparison operators, and boolean operators. In addition, you will need to use the modulo operator (%).

Hints

If the problem description sounded confusing, then start by listing all integers that are within 2 of the integer 10.

Solution

An integer n is within two of a multiple of ten if its last digit is an 8, 9, 0, 1, or 2. Having established that, we only need to express this in code, for instance by specifying two ranges. Thus, we check that n % 10 is at least 8, and also add a check that it is at most 2. One of those two checks has to be fulfilled, so we combine them with the disjunction operator. Refer to Listing 313 for the code.

```
1 public boolean nearTen(int n) {
2   return n % 10 >= 8 || n % 10 <= 2;
3 }
```

Listing 313: nearTen – solution

teenSum

Problem

The function teenSum takes two integers a and b as its input. If at least one of those numbers is in the range [13 ... 19] return 19. Otherwise, return the sum of a and b. The code skeleton is provided in Listing 314.

```
1 public int teenSum(int a, int b) {
2 // your code here
3 }
```

Listing 314: teenSum – skeleton

Tools

You can use conditional statements, comparison operators, boolean operators, and arithmetic operators.

Hints

Start by determining whether the value of the integer a is in the specified range.

Solution

This is a very straightforward problem. We first check if a is in the range [13 ... 19], then we do the same with b. If any of those conditions are met, we return 19. Otherwise, we return the sum of a and b. Refer to Listing 315 for the code.

```
1  public int teenSum(int a, int b) {
2    if (a >= 13 && a <= 19 || b >= 13 && b <= 19) {
3      return 19;
4    }
5    return a + b;
6  }
```

Listing 315: teenSum – solution

answerCell

Problem

The function `answerCell` takes three booleans `isMorning`, `isMom`, and `isAsleep` as its input. If `isAsleep` is true, return false. If `isMorning` is true, return true if `isMom` is true, and `false` otherwise. In all remaining cases, return true. The code skeleton is provided in Listing 316.

```
1 public boolean answerCell(boolean isMorning,
2                           boolean isMom,
3                           boolean isAsleep) {
4 // your code here
5 }
```

Listing 316: `answerCell` – skeleton

Tools

You can use conditional statements, comparison operators, and boolean operators.

Hints

Translate the problem description sentence by sentence into code.

Solution

While this problem might appear a bit complicated, it is not if you approach it in a methodological manner. First, we know that if isAsleep is true, we return false. Otherwise, if isMorning is true, we return true if isMom is true and false otherwise. As a catch-all statement, we return true. Refer to Listing 317 for the code.

```java
public boolean answerCell(boolean isMorning,
                         boolean isMom,
                         boolean isAsleep) {
  if (isAsleep) {
    return false;
  } else {
    if (isMorning) {
      if (isMom) {
        return true;
      } else {
        return false;
      }
    }
  }
  return true;
}
```

Listing 317: answerCell – solution

Discussion

As you can probably see, this code could be simplified. The value isMom is a boolean, and we return the value of that boolean. Thus, we can as well just return isMom right away. In addition, the nesting of the if-statements can be broken up. See Listing 318 for a cleaner variation of the solution.

```java
public boolean answerCell(boolean isMorning,
                         boolean isMom,
                         boolean isAsleep) {
  if (isAsleep) return false;
  if (isMorning) return isMom;
  return true;
}
```

Listing 318: answerCell – variation

281

teaParty

Problem

The function `teaParty` takes two integers `tea` and `candy` as its input. It returns an integer that indicates how good your tea party is, ranging from bad (0) to good (1) to great (2). The tea party is good if both `candy` and `tea` are greater than 5. However, if one of the input values is at least twice as high as the other, the party is great. Lastly, if the value of either input variable is less than five, the party is bad. The code skeleton is provided in Listing 319.

```
1 public int teaParty(int tea, int candy) {
2 // your code here
3 }
```

Listing 319: teaParty – skeleton

Tools

You can use conditional statements, comparison operators, and boolean operators.

Hints

Keep in mind that there are two top-level cases. Either both `candy` and `tea` are both at least 5, or at least one of them is less than 5.

Solution

There are two cases. Either both input variables are at least 5, or at least one of them is less than 5. If this sounds confusing to you, use the number line to visualize it. In the first case, the party is at least good (1), so we need to add checks to determine if it is great (2), which is the case if one of the input variables is at least twice as large as the other. The second case is triggered if at least one of the input variables is less than 5. In that case, we return 0, which is also the value we return as a default. See Listing 320 for the code.

```java
public int teaParty(int tea, int candy) {
  if (candy >= 5 && tea >= 5) {
    if (candy >= 2 * tea  ) return 2;
    if (tea   >= 2 * candy) return 2;
    return 1;
  }
  if (candy < 5 || tea < 5) return 0;
  return 0;
}
```

Listing 320: teaParty – solution

Discussion

You have hopefully noticed that there is a redundancy in Listing 320. If this is not clear by analyzing the range of the variables, then look at the return values. We have two conditions that return 0. Thus, we can get rid of the second if-statement altogether. See Listing 321 for the final code.

```java
public int teaParty(int tea, int candy) {
  if (candy >= 5 && tea >= 5) {
    if (candy >= 2 * tea  ) return 2;
    if (tea   >= 2 * candy) return 2;
    return 1;
  }
  return 0;
}
```

Listing 321: teaParty – variation

fizzString

Problem

The function `fizzString` takes a string `str` as its input. If `str` starts with 'f' and ends with 'b', return "FizzBuzz". If it starts with 'f', return "Fizz". If it ends with 'b', return "Buzz". As the default value, return the input string unchanged. The code skeleton is provided in Listing 322.

```
1 public String fizzString(String str) {
2 // your code here
3 }
```

Listing 322: `fizzString` – skeleton

Tools

You can use conditional statements, comparison operators, and boolean operators. In addition, you will have to use the string methods `charAt` and `length`. Alternatively, you may use the string methods `startsWith` and `endsWith`.

Hints

Start by declaring and initializing two boolean variables that record whether the input string `str` starts with an 'f' as well as ends with a 'b'.

Solution

We first declare two boolean variables. The first one records whether the input string `str` starts with an `'f'`, the second one whether it ends with a `'b'`. Afterwards, we construct three if-statements that record the conditions that were specified in the problem statement. As we return a string right away in those if-statements, the first check has to consider both conditions. As the default value, we return `str` unchanged. See Listing 323 for the code.

```
1 public String fizzString(String str) {
2   boolean fizz = str.charAt(0) == 'f';
3   boolean buzz = str.charAt(str.length() - 1) == 'b';
4   if (fizz && buzz) return "FizzBuzz";
5   if (fizz) return "Fizz";
6   if (buzz) return "Buzz";
7   return str;
8 }
```

Listing 323: fizzString – solution

Discussion

An alternative solution consists of successively building a string `acc`, used as an accumulator, which we may return. In that case, we do not need to check that both conditions are fulfilled. Instead, we optionally concatenate `acc` successively with `"Fizz"` and `"Buzz"`. However, afterwards, we have to check that the accumulator is not empty as we will have to return the input string `str` in that case. See Listing 324 for the corresponding code. That code also uses the string methods `startsWith` and `endsWith`.

```
1 public String fizzString(String str) {
2   boolean fizz = str.startsWith("f");
3   boolean buzz = str.endsWith("b");
4   String acc = "";
5   if (fizz) acc += "Fizz";
6   if (buzz) acc += "Buzz";
7   return (acc.equals("")) ? str : acc;
8 }
```

Listing 324: fizzString – variation

fizzString2

Problem

The function `fizzString2` takes an integer n as its input. If n is a multiple of both 3 and 5, return "FizzBuzz". If n is a multiple of 3, return "Fizz". If n is a multiple of 5, return "Buzz". As the default value, return the input as a string, followed by an exclamation mark, e.g. if the input is 1, the output is "1!". The code skeleton is provided in Listing 325.

```
1 public String fizzString2(int n) {
2 // your code here
3 }
```

Listing 325: fizzString2 – skeleton

Tools

You can use conditional statements, comparison operators, and boolean operators. In addition, you will have to use the modulo operator.

Hints

This problem is very similar to the previous one. Furthermore, keep in mind that Java converts an integer to a string if you concatenate it with another string. For instance, the result of the expression 1 + "!" is "1!".

Solution

We first declare two boolean variables. The first one records whether the input integer n is a multiple of 3, the second one whether it is a multiple of 5. Afterwards, we construct three if-statements that record the conditions that were specified in the problem statement. As we return a string right away, the first check has to consider both conditions. Finally, if none of the conditions are met, we return the input, converted to a string, and appended with an exclamation mark. See Listing 326 for the code.

```
1  public String fizzString2(int n) {
2    boolean fizz = n % 3 == 0;
3    boolean buzz = n % 5 == 0;
4    if (fizz && buzz) return "FizzBuzz!";
5    if (fizz) return "Fizz!";
6    if (buzz) return "Buzz!";
7    return n + "!";
8  }
```

Listing 326: fizzString2 – solution

Discussion

Just like with the last problem, there is a more elegant variation. There is a twist, though. We know that the string we return always ends with an exclamation mark, which means that the difference is the preceding string. Thus, we build an accumulator acc, which we swap with the input integer in the return statement if it is empty. See Listing 327 for the corresponding code.

```
1  public String fizzString2(int n) {
2    boolean fizz = n % 3 == 0;
3    boolean buzz = n % 5 == 0;
4    String acc = "";
5    if (fizz) acc += "Fizz";
6    if (buzz) acc += "Buzz";
7    return (acc.equals("") ? n : acc) + "!";
8  }
```

Listing 327: fizzString2 – variation

twoAsOne

Problem

The function `twoAsOne` takes three integers a, b, and c as its input. Return `true` if two of those integers are equal to the remaining one, and `false` otherwise. The code skeleton is provided in Listing 328.

```
1 public boolean twoAsOne(int a, int b, int c) {
2 // your code here
3 }
```

Listing 328: twoAsOne – skeleton

Tools

You can use conditional statements, comparison operators, boolean operators, and arithmetic operators.

Hints

How many ways are there to add two out of three numbers?

Solution

There are three ways to sum up two out of three numbers, if the order is not important. They are a + b, a + c, and b + c. Thus, we check if any of those three sums is equal to the input element that is not part of that sum. See Listing 329 for the code.

```
1 public boolean twoAsOne(int a, int b, int c) {
2    return a + b == c || a + c == b || b + c == a;
3 }
```

Listing 329: twoAsOne – solution

inOrder

Problem

The function inOrder takes three integers a, b, and c as its input. Return true if two of those integers are equal to the remaining one, and false otherwise. The code skeleton is provided in Listing 330.

```
1 public boolean inOrder(int a, int b, int c, boolean bOk) {
2 // your code here
3 }
```

Listing 330: *inOrder – skeleton*

Tools

You can use conditional statements, comparison operators, and boolean operators.

Hints

At this point, this problem should be easy for you.

Solution

There are two cases: bOk is either true or false. In the former case, we only need to check that b < c, in the latter that a < b < c. Of course, that expression has to be split into a < b and b < c. See Listing 331 for the code.

```
1 public boolean inOrder(int a, int b, int c, boolean bOk) {
2   if (bOk) {
3     return b < c;
4   }
5   return a < b && b < c;
6 }
```

Listing 331: inOrder – solution

Discussion

There are some simplifications we could do. The first one is using the ternary operator, as in Listing 332. The parentheses are redundant, and were added for readability.

```
1 public boolean inOrder(int a, int b, int c, boolean bOk) {
2   return bOk ? (b < c) : (a < b && b < c);
3 }
```

Listing 332: inOrder – variation 1

There is still some repetition, as you can see. In both cases, we check whether b < c. We can remove that as well by making that check conditional. For this, though, we flip the check of the condition bOk to make the comparison a < b optional. See Listing 333 for the code.

```
1 public boolean inOrder(int a, int b, int c, boolean bOk) {
2   return (!bOk ?  a < b : true) && (b < c);
3 }
```

Listing 333: inOrder – variation 2

inOrderEqual

Problem

The function inOrder takes three integers a, b, c as well as a boolean equalOk as its input. If equalOk is true, return true if it is the case that a <= b <= c, and false otherwise. If equalOk is false, return true if a < b < c, and false otherwise. The code skeleton is provided in Listing 334.

```
1 public boolean inOrderEqual(int a, int b, int c,
2                             boolean equalOk) {
3 // your code here
4 }
```

Listing 334: inOrderEqual – skeleton

Tools

You can use conditional statements, comparison operators, and boolean operators.

Hints

This is straightforward. Translate the problem description line-by-line into code.

Solution

There are two cases: `equalOk` is either `true` or `false`. In the former case, we check that a <= b <= c, in the latter, we check that a < b < c. Both expressions have to be spit up, though. See Listing 335 for the code.

```
1 public boolean inOrderEqual(int a, int b, int c,
2                             boolean equalOk) {
3   if (equalOk) {
4     return a <= b && b <= c;
5   }
6   return a < b && b < c;
7 }
```

Listing 335: inOrderEqual – solution

lastDigit

Problem

The function `lastDigit` takes three integers a, b, and c as its input. Return `true` if at least two of them have the same last digit, and `false` otherwise. The code skeleton is provided in Listing 336.

```
1 public boolean lastDigit(int a, int b, int c) {
2 // your code here
3 }
```

Listing 336: lastDigit – skeleton

Tools

You can use conditional statements, comparison operators, and boolean operators. You will also have to use the modulo operator.

Hints

Listing all possible last digits and counting if two or more of the input integers have the same last digit is one approach, but that would hardly be ideal. Instead, use comparisons. For instance, if a and b have the same last digit, then a % 10 is equal to b % 10.

Solution

Instead of trying to determine if two or more of the tree input integers a, b, and c have the same last digit, we can just as well take all combinations of two of those three integers and determine if they share the last integer by computing their modulo of 10. There are three such combinations: a and b, a and c, b and c. After comparing their respective last digits, we build a disjunction. See Listing 337 for the code.

```
1  public boolean lastDigit(int a, int b, int c) {
2     return a % 10 == b % 10
3            || a % 10 == c % 10
4            || b % 10 == c % 10;
5  }
```

Listing 337: lastDigit – solution

lessBy10

Problem

The function `lessBy10` takes three integers a, b, and c as its input. Return `true` if the absolute difference of two of those values differs by 10 or more, and `false` otherwise. The code skeleton is provided in Listing 338.

```
1 public boolean lessBy10(int a, int b, int c) {
2 // your code here
3 }
```

Listing 338: lessBy10 – skeleton

Tools

You can use conditional statements, comparison operators, and boolean operators. Furthermore, you can use the method `Math.abs`.

Hints

This problem is similar to the last one, `lastDigit`. In fact, it is a simpler variation of it. Again, there are three possible combinations. Go through each of them and check if their absolute difference is 10 or more. Also, the goal is to find out if one or more of the combinations of input values meets that condition, not exactly one.

Solution

There are three combinations of the input values a, b, and c: a and b, a and c, and b and c. For each combination, we check if their absolute difference amounts to at least 10. We put disjunction operators between those checks as we need to determine if one or more of those combinations fulfill the stated criterion. See Listing 339 for the code.

```java
1 public boolean lessBy10(int a, int b, int c) {
2   return Math.abs(a - c) >= 10
3          || Math.abs(a - b) >= 10
4          || Math.abs(b - c) >= 10;
5 }
```

Listing 339: lessBy10 – solution

withoutDoubles

Problem

The function withoutDoubles takes two integers die1 and die2 as well as a boolean noDoubles as its input. The integers represent six-sided dice. Return the sum of die1 and die2, except when noDoubles is true. In that case, increment the value of one of the dice by 1 before returning their sum. Of course, if the value of that die is 6, it has to be changed to 1. The code skeleton is provided in Listing 340.

```
1 public int withoutDoubles(int die1, int die2,
2                           boolean noDoubles) {
3 // your code here
4 }
```

Listing 340: *withoutDoubles – skeleton*

Tools

You can use conditional statements, comparison operators, and boolean operators. Furthermore, you may want to use the modulo operator.

Hints

This problem is similar to the last one, lastDigit. In fact, it is a simpler variation of it. Again, there are three possible combinations. Go through each of them and check if their absolute difference is 10 or more. Also, the goal is to find out if one or more of the combinations of input values meets that condition, not exactly one.

Solution

We first check if noDoubles is true. If that is the case and the integers die1 and die2 are equal, we modify one of those integers. However, we have to keep in mind that a 6 flips over to a 1, while all other values are incremented by 1. As the goal is to return the sum of the two integers, it does not matter whether we increase the first or second one. Thus, we adjust one of the integers as needed. See Listing 341 for the code. You may wonder why we compare only die1 to 6. Well, in the body of that if-statement both integers are equal, so if die1 is equal to 6, die2 is equal to 6 as well.

```
1 public int withoutDoubles(int die1, int die2,
2                           boolean noDoubles) {
3   if (noDoubles && (die1 == die2)) {
4     return (die1 == 6) ? 1 + die2 : (die1 + 1) + die2;
5   }
6   return die1 + die2;
7 }
```

Listing 341: withoutDoubles – solution

Discussion

Perhaps surprisingly, there are some interesting variations to the solution shown in Listing 341. First, we may want to modify die1 in-place instead of returning a sum right away. This leads to more concise code, as can be seen in Listing 342.

```
1 public int withoutDoubles(int die1, int die2,
2                           boolean noDoubles) {
3   if (noDoubles && (die1 == die2)) {
4     die1 = (die1 == 6) ? 1 : die1 + 1;
5   }
6   return die1 + die2;
7 }
```

Listing 342: withoutDoubles – variation1

There is more that can be done. Maybe you noticed that we repeat the integer 1 in the body of the if-statement. This is, in general, poor style, but a good argument could be made that it does not really matter in our case. Still, factoring it out makes the code a bit cleaner. Have a look at the code in Listing 343 to see for yourself. It also leads to an even more elegant simplification.

```
1  public int withoutDoubles(int die1, int die2,
2                            boolean noDoubles) {
3    if (noDoubles && (die1 == die2)) {
4      die1 = 1 + ((die1 == 6) ? 0 : die1);
5    }
6    return die1 + die2;
7  }
```

Listing 343: withoutDoubles – variation2

Does the modified code remind you of something? For instance, is there a way to get rid of the ternary operator? Indeed there is. You can replace that code with the modulo operator. Thus, via a number of successive transformations, we have arrived at a clean and very elegant solution, which can be seen in Listing 344.

```
1  public int withoutDoubles(int die1, int die2,
2                            boolean noDoubles) {
3    if (noDoubles && (die1 == die2)) {
4      die1 = 1 + die1 % 6;
5    }
6    return die1 + die2;
7  }
```

Listing 344: withoutDoubles – variation3

maxMod5

Problem

The function maxMod5 takes two integers a and b as its input. If both values are identical, return 0. If both have the same remainder when divided by 5, return the minimum of both values. Otherwise, return their maximum. The code skeleton is provided in Listing 345.

```
1 public int maxMod5(int a, int b) {
2 // your code here
3 }
```

Listing 345: maxMod5 – skeleton

Tools

You can use conditional statements, comparison operators, and boolean operators. Furthermore, you may want to use the modulo operator. For convenience, feel free to use the methods Math.min and Math.max.

Hints

This is a straightforward problem. There are three different cases to consider, so tackle them one after the other.

Solution

There are three cases, which we take care of sequentially. First, if a equals b, we return 0. Second, if a % 5 is equal to b % 5, we return the minimum of a and b. Third, if the function has not returned yet, we now return the maximum of a and b. See Listing 346 for the code.

```java
1 public int maxMod5(int a, int b) {
2    if (a == b)          return 0;
3    if (a % 5 == b % 5) return Math.min(a, b);
4    return Math.max(a, b);
5 }
```

Listing 346: maxMod5 – solution

redTicket

Problem

The function `redTicket` takes three integers a, b, and c as its input. If all values are identical and equal to 2, return 10. If they are all identical but not equal to 2, return 5. If a is not identical to both b and c, return 1. Otherwise, return 0. The code skeleton is provided in Listing 347.

```
1 public int redTicket(int a, int b, int c) {
2 // your code here
3 }
```

Listing 347: `redTicket` – skeleton

Tools

You can use conditional statements, comparison operators, and boolean operators.

Hints

Keep in mind that if a is equal to b, and b is equal to c, then a is equal to c.

Solution

The problem description can be translated into code line-by-line. First, we use an if-statement to check if all values are identical. If that is the case, we use another if-statement to determine whether to return 10 or 5. The former happens if a is equal to 2, the latter in all other cases. Lastly, we use another if-statement to determine whether a is different from both b and c. If that is the case, we return 1, and 0 otherwise. See Listing 348 for the code.

```java
public int redTicket(int a, int b, int c) {
  if (a == b && b == c) {
    return (a == 2) ? 10 : 5;
  }
  return (a != b && a != c) ? 1 : 0;
}
```

Listing 348: `redTicket` – solution

greenTicket

Problem

The function `greenTicket` takes three integers a, b, and c as its input. If all values are different from each other, return 0. If they are all identical, return 20. If two of the provided values are identical, return 10. The code skeleton is provided in Listing 349.

```
1 public int greenTicket(int a, int b, int c) {
2 // your code here
3 }
```

Listing 349: greenTicket – skeleton

Tools

You can use conditional statements, comparison operators, and boolean operators.

Hints

This problem is similar to the preceding one, `redTicket`. Again, keep in mind that if a is equal to b, and b is equal to c, then a is equal to c.

Solution

First, we will take care of the easy case and use an if-statement to determine if all of the provided values a, b, and c are different from each other. There are many ways to tackle this. For instance, we could compare a with b and c, and check that they are not identical. Afterwards, we compare b and c to ensure those values are not identical either. If those conditions are met, we return 0. Otherwise, we check that all values are identical. For this, we need to only compare a and b as well as b and c. If all values are identical, we return 20.

Afterwards, we need to check if two values are identical. This is not entirely trivial. However, here is an important insight: We have already checked whether all values are different, but also whether they are all the same. In the first case, there is three times one integer with the same value, in the second there are three integers with the same value. This implies that the last case, which consists of two integers with the same value, can be covered with a final catch-all statement that returns 10. See Listing 350 for the code.

```
1 public int greenTicket(int a, int b, int c) {
2   if (a != b && a != c && c != b) return 0;
3   if (a == b && b == c)           return 20;
4   return 10;
5 }
```

Listing 350: greenTicket – solution

blueTicket

Problem

The function blueTicket takes three integers a, b, and c as its input. If any two of those values sum up to 10, return 10. If the sum of a and b is ten less than the sum of b and c, or if it is ten less than the sum of a and c, return 5. Otherwise, return 0. The code skeleton is provided in Listing 351.

```
1 public int blueTicket(int a, int b, int c) {
2 // your code here
3 }
```

Listing 351: blueTicket – skeleton

Tools

You can use conditional statements, comparison operators, boolean operators, and arithmetic operators.

Hints

This problem is similar to the preceding two.

Solution

We have seen a few quite similar problems already, so this one will not pose a problem. We first check if any of the sums a + b, a + c, and b + c sum up to 10. If so, we return 10. Afterwards, we check if a + b == b + c + 10 or if a + b = a + c + 10. If any of those conditions hold, we return 5. Otherwise, we return 0. For the sake of readability, it is justifiable to store the various sums just mentioned in helper variables. See Listing 352 for the code.

```
1 public int blueTicket(int a, int b, int c) {
2     int ab = a + b;
3     int ac = a + c;
4     int bc = b + c;
5     if (ab == 10 || ac == 10 || bc == 10) return 10;
6     if (ab == bc + 10 || ab == ac + 10)    return 5;
7     return 0;
8 }
```

Listing 352: blueTicket – solution

Discussion

If you look at the code, you may notice a simplification. If it is not obvious, take a look at this equation again: a + b = b + c + 10. Can you find a shorter equivalent expression? Well, of course we can just subtract b from both sides! For the sake of completeness, the final solution is given in Listing 353.

```
1 public int blueTicket(int a, int b, int c) {
2     int ab = a + b;
3     int ac = a + c;
4     int bc = b + c;
5     if (ab == 10 || ac == 10 || bc == 10) return 10;
6     if (a == c + 10 || b == c + 10)        return 5;
7     return 0;
8 }
```

Listing 353: blueTicket – variation

shareDigit

Problem

The function shareDigit takes two integers a and b as its input, which each consist of two digits. Return true if those two integers have at least one digit in common, and false otherwise. The code skeleton is provided in Listing 354.

```
1 public boolean shareDigit(int a, int b) {
2 // your code here
3 }
```

Listing 354: shareDigit – skeleton

Tools

You can use conditional statements, comparison operators, boolean operators, arithmetic operators, and the modulo operator.

Hints

You have to extract the place value of each integer. To get the first digit, divide by 10, and to get the second one, use the modulo operator.

Solution

We start by extracting the first and second digit of the integers a and b. Afterwards, we check all possible pairs for equality. Thus, we compare the first digit of a with the first and second digit of b. Afterwards, we compare the second digit of a with the first and second digit of b. If any of the conditions has been met, we return true. Otherwise, we return false. See Listing 355 for the code.

```
1 public boolean shareDigit(int a, int b) {
2    int a1 = a / 10;
3    int a2 = a % 10;
4    int b1 = b / 10;
5    int b2 = b % 10;
6    return a1 == b1 || a1 == b2
7           || a2 == b1 || a2 == b2;
8 }
```

Listing 355: shareDigit – solution

sumLimit

Problem

The function sumLimit takes two non-negative integers a and b as its input. If their sum has the same number of digits as the integer a, return their sum. Otherwise, return a. The code skeleton is provided in Listing 356.

```
1 public int sumLimit(int a, int b) {
2 // your code here
3 }
```

Listing 356: sumLimit – skeleton

Tools

You can use conditional statements, comparison operators, arithmetic operators, and the following string methods: valueOf and length.

Hints

The string method valueOf converts an integer to a string, e.g. String.valueOf(1) results in "1". Thus, in order to determine the number of digits of a non-negative integer, we convert it to a string and then compute the length of the resulting string.

Solution

First we convert the sum of a and b into an integer. Afterwards, we compute the length of that string. Then, we do the same with the integer a. Finally, we compare the length of both strings. If it is identical, we return the sum of a and b. Otherwise, we return a. See Listing 357 for the code.

```
public int sumLimit(int a, int b) {
  int length_ab = String.valueOf(a + b).length();
  int length_a  = String.valueOf(a).length();
  return (length_ab == length_a) ? a + b : a;
}
```

Listing 357: sumLimit – solution